Paul Newman

Biography

An Extraordinary Life

Alexandra E Eersteling

TABLE OF CONTENTS

CHAPTER I

I'm in my Connecticut home, in the library, on a formal small couch by the fire. I had just smoked a marijuana and remembered the entire map of my childhood hometown of Shaker Heights, Ohio. It's all there to be remembered, things I thought were long gone, things I never expected to remember...

In 1925, I was born there. Shaker Heights was then the Cleveland suburb to which every other American suburb aspired. It was the yardstick by which other prosperous areas were measured. We lived in a large three-story house on Brighton Road, which was not the wealthiest street in the neighbourhood, but we were clearly well-off. My father, Arthur, and his brother, Joe (known as J.S., and a prolific creator of popular doggerel in his spare time), ran the Newman-Stern sporting-goods company from an imposing corner building downtown; it was second only to New York's original Abercrombie & Fitch in its category.

As a child growing up in Shaker Heights, I recall horse-drawn carriages pulling milk trucks or ice blocks. Our public schools were regarded as the best in the country. We had hundreds of acres of woods and five small lakes to fish and explore. Safety was never an issue; you could spend four days in those woods in the summer and nothing bad would happen to you. The most boisterous it got was when we kids conducted a "war"; we'd steal people's tomato plant stakes and use them as spears, defending ourselves with garbage-can lids. It was like a Papua New Guinean rite.

In the calm streets and estates, all the families were lily white; there were no immigrants or Black people. The Newmans were possibly the first Jewish family to settle on Brighton Road. But we were exactly like everyone else; we'd set up fake circuses in our backyard, selling lemonade and performing sophisticated swing routines. Young children my age and my elder brother, Art Jr., would visit my house, and our father would entertain them by telling them made-up stories featuring his creations, the ever-adventurous Terry Berry Boys. He'd tell them in a series, a new chapter every night. When he was done, he'd pretend to be a scary animal, and all the neighbourhood kids would jump on top of him and wrestle with him. He'd cover up like a boxer, and then it'd be over. "That's the end, guys," he'd say, and the kids would be led back to their respective homes, leaving Art and me to sleep. Of course, Art would always find time to kick the bejesus out of me, frequently in what we referred to as "the club"-actually, our home's third-floor "attic," where we shared a playroom.

He'd like sitting on my back, grabbing hold of my chin, and seeing how far he could bend my neck back. I guess he thought I deserved it because he thought I was getting all the attention from our mother, Tress, and all of her devotion, while he was getting crumbs. Arthur and I were very different in that our various relationships with our mothers didn't upset him in the end. Arthur always believed that, of all the options accessible to him, God had placed him in a position where nothing could be better. My brother decided to remember the positive aspects of our childhood, but I prefer to recall the mistakes and missteps.

We spent a lot of time up in our playroom doing our assignments. Art rehearsed his drums there as well, while I listened to records on the Victrola and relaxed in a comfy chair reading comic books. Our "club" was more welcoming than our family's elegant living room downstairs, where no one actually lived. My sense of "decoration" may have begun right there in that nicely equipped showplace. My mother took tremendous delight in the appearance of that living room; to me, her taste was frigid, sort of "Bloomingdale's Modern." Everything was perfectly manicured; everything was built for looks rather than comfort. She made the decision to lay all-black carpeting early on, and then got herself a white Spitz dog because it looked fantastic on the carpet. Of course, the dog created a trail of white fur wherever he went.

Next to the living room was a proper dining room, where we ate almost all of our meals together for years; there was rarely any discussion, and evenings at the table could be agonising. Our dining table was inlaid and always had a linen tablecloth on it. Every night, it would be set with exquisite china. My father was typically the last to come, so we'd be sitting there. He usually wore a jacket and tie, but if he had time to change after work, he'd wear a bathrobe. Despite the fact that we had a maid, my mother passed the plates around herself, frequently offering some very simply cooked meat, veggies, and mashed potatoes. My father would normally propose some type of toast before we started, and my brother and I would clink our water glasses.

My mother eventually decided she didn't want to iron that linen tablecloth any longer, so she had us eat in the much smaller breakfast room off the kitchen. My father objected to the change, so he continued to eat alone in the dining room. Dessert would be pudding or cake-my mother was an excellent baker-and then Father would say "Excuse me" and go upstairs to read (he never tired of the Encyclopaedia Britannica, which he read end to end several times) or snooze. Art and I would help with the dishes before going up to our playroom to make popcorn and drink iced tea or pop.

Art and I would also knock our heads on the wall in the dining room. Literally. We did it in secret until the dent became noticeable to my parents. This was no tippy-toe banging; this was a violent whacking that knocked the plaster behind the wall covering down. We had to have fucked our brains out. It was our personal Wailing Wall. I couldn't vent my wrath on somebody my size, so I took it out on the wall. It makes me giggle now to think of us, these two small kids touching each other on the shoulder and saying, "My turn."…"Oh, after you!" Because Art was bigger, he most likely received the

5

opening shot. We never banged in the same location because his head was about six inches higher than mine. (When I returned home after WWII, I checked on the wall and was astounded to find the massive ruptures.)

Our home was filled with the noises of incessant battle. It may be a quiet conflict, like the slicing of knives through human flesh, as stealthy and stalking as commandos creeping stealthily through the night. It may also be explosive and raucous, which was frequently the case when my mother erupted. Alternatively, threatening to erupt. We'd sit there waiting for something to go wrong, for someone to slip off the eggshells and flee, for a mistake and the ensuing explosion. We'd be in bed when we heard our parents yelling at each other. I'd hear things crack. My mother once grabbed a picture from the wall and broke it over the top of my father's head during a disagreement. It was a pastel of naked nymphs (which I had viewed with a magnifying glass several times). It hung directly over the living room sofa. My father was probably left strolling around with the frame wrapped around his shoulders. I'm sure there was significant grief, but all I can think about today are cartoon depictions of these things.

***

America began the Great Depression when I was five years old. During those years, 85 percent of the sporting-goods stores in the country went bankrupt, and my father appeared despondent. We were a luxury store during a period when no one was purchasing premium products. Newman-Stern would hold a sale, and whether or not it was successful would determine whether or not we would remain open. My father went to Chicago and got the Spalding and Wilson companies to extend him $250,000 worth of merchandise on consignment; because my father had such a good reputation for integrity, the manufacturers knew they'd eventually get paid back for their goods. It was a remarkable credit to my father and uncle Joe and their business ethics that they made it through the Great Depression financially unscathed.

We all pitched in. My father would never let my mother work, but she still let the maid go, which enraged him. Then she responded, "I'll clean, and I'll take the money I was paying the maid and buy the kind of furniture I want." That she did. She did all of the laundry, mangling, and ironing, bought new furniture or reupholster old furniture herself, and even stitched the draperies and valances. (It was a source of pleasure for my father, as well as a triumph of appearances, that he never allowed our membership at the Jewish country club, the Oakwood, lapse.)

I started out at the Newman-Stern stockroom, but as I grew older, I was transferred to the sales floor. I sold anything from binoculars to tennis equipment. I was a competent salesman, a trustworthy salesman. If I were selling a bowling ball to a guy and he replied, "Golly, I really don't know if I need a new bowling ball," I'd tell him, "If you don't need it, don't buy it." I had a good time working there.

Following WWII, Newman-Stern also sold army surplus. A man had dropped by peddling crates of discarded Norden bombsights, the futuristic, once-top-secret military technology that allowed US planes to drop payloads on Germany and Japan with pinpoint accuracy. Understandably, this individual couldn't get rid of his bulky goods. "What can anyone use this thing for?" you'd think when you saw these intricate contraptions. But Uncle Joe (who had studied applied science in college) and my father began disassembling the devices and solving the conundrum. There was a section of the bombsight where pressing a small button activated a powerful electric motor, and with a little tinkering, you might have yourself a reasonably priced automated garage-door opener. There were rheostats that could be repurposed for a variety of vital domestic applications, and an early analog computer was included.

The brothers purchased a full-page ad in the Cleveland Plain Dealer, outlining how each of the bombsight's thirty-six individual components might be recycled. You couldn't get into our store for three or four days. Cleveland's prestigious Case School called and purchased two full units for $2,800 each-a huge sum at the time. It was chaos-perhaps $200,000 in revenue for a few days.

Uncle Joe and my father were overjoyed. It wasn't so much the money as it was the fact that they had taken something that had been provided everywhere and only they had the vision to grasp its potential. They'd created a great hit. This was the allure of shopping. And the Newman brothers were romantics.

It hadn't begun that way, at least not for my father. My father aspired to be a writer when he was younger; that was all he wanted to do. Soon after returning from World War I, he was employed as the Cleveland Press's youngest reporter ever. Brother Joe, on the other hand, persuaded him to join his budding sporting-goods business, which had originally specialised in selling electrical-experiment kits for boys as well as more advanced microphones, transmitters, and telegraphs. (The huge shift to sporting goods occurred after the government prohibited the selling of private telegraphy equipment following America's declaration of war on the Kaiser in 1917.) Joe was the firm's president, and my father was the secretary-treasurer, both of whom were overshadowed by my uncle. He couldn't see a way out-he was just starting a family, he had obligations, and he was a good man. He couldn't bear the entire financial load on his young wife, and Arthur Newman Sr. never believed in divorce.

He became a prisoner, imprisoned by the store, imprisoned by his dick, with little time to consider his options. I don't believe his efforts eventually satisfied him. I doubt his castle satisfied him. I'm not sure his family delighted him either.

***

Teresa Fetzko, my mother, was a lovely young woman who came here with her family from Eastern Europe (what was then the collapsing Austro-Hungarian Empire, now known as Slovakia). She arrived not long after the turn of the century, basically a girl dressed in rags. Her family was impoverished, which led to my mother's constant worry of losing everything. Her father was a bricklayer, not a professor, as she claimed. Her mother died while she was a youngster, and when she was sixteen, she married a young man, but divorced him soon after because, she claimed, he assaulted her.

When my father met her, she was working as a ticket taker at Cleveland's Alhambra Theatre. Going on a date with my father, who was far more accomplished than she was, she decided to change from Roman Catholicism to Christian Science, which was less problematic (and probably less familiar to her beau's Jewish family). My father soon got her pregnant, and despite a lot of pressure from his family, the baby (my brother, Art Jr.) was born, and Arthur Sr. and Tress married later. My father did it under duress, and I believe that if he hadn't been such a good guy, he would have abandoned her in an instant. I'm not sure if it was because my mother adored him, because she despised abortion, or for other reasons, but the two of them managed to settle down together. I was born roughly a year after Art Jr., whose impending birth allegedly sparked substantial debate about alternate alternatives.

Tress was viewed negatively by the Newman family from the start for a variety of reasons. Because she was a Gentile and they were Jews, albeit generally non observant ones. Because she was stunning. Because they thought she was a hussy ("Wasn't she a divorcée?"), a gold digger, and beneath their social and educational station (ironic, given that the Newmans themselves were itinerant peddlers and tinkers only one generation removed). They thought my mother's people were an embarrassment. How inferior she must have felt, and how excluded he must have felt!

My father was a quiet man who, from what I recall, never interacted with his wife's family. My mother took my brother and me to see our dour and silent grandfather every other week (where we were fed his wife's excellent chicken soup), but my father never attended; I believe he only saw them twice. I also believe my father was upset with us because we always went to see our grandparents on Sundays; my father worked six days a week, and our visits left him home alone. Sunday, in fact, was the least enjoyable day of the week for him. Still, my father didn't want anything to do with them; I'm not even sure he ever let them into our house. They were the unfortunate relatives.

It's not strange, however, that my mother grew into a very private person with only a few close friends. And, while she was committed to her home and her husband, she eventually detested them and distrusted her entire family. She was the most sceptical woman who had ever lived, hysterical by the prospect of never being accepted or getting her fair share of anything. And those doubts followed us for the rest of our lives.

What my mother did embrace were her own passionate passions-but never the goods that inspired them. She developed an interest in opera, for example, and would bring me to five-hour Wagner performances at Severance Hall, where the music would elicit a soaring response from her. She enjoyed the huge flood of feelings that poured through her, whether it was tears or excitement, as a child, when I did something cute or came downstairs looking very attractive, wearing small shorts and a sweater. The youngster himself was not seen, and neither was the opera heard. What transpired inside her thoughts and heart had nothing to do with Wagner or me, but just with her own bliss. You could only hope she'd let you leave. And if the child had been able to pull away or the music had stopped, she wouldn't have missed either of them; her emotions would have raged on, fueled by their own magnitude and scale, until they died of fatigue. Only then might she have inquired, "Where is he?" ? "Did someone turn off the music?"

Sexually, you could probably take her partner away and the intensity would have continued until she came in and questioned, "Where'd he go?" That's a terrible thing to say about your mother, I know, but I think it's hilarious-and tragic.

In my mind's eye, I'm a youngster in anguish with a splinter in my finger, and my mother surrounds me, cooing and struggling and probing until the life of this little wretch is squeezed out of him. "But I was only trying to comfort the poor thing!" she exclaims as she discovers the lifeless figure in her arms.

I was like one of her poor fucking dogs who had cancer and were so big they couldn't move, and my mother kept feeding them chocolates until she killed them with love. My mother was completely unaware of the harm she was causing. Her desire to shower affection not only exceeded the item on which she showered attention, but also had nothing to do with that object. My mother's dogs were analogous to her children, to the orphaned core trying to protect himself from being crushed by the ornamentation. It took fifty years for the core to sit down and start dealing with it.

She never saw the dogs, only her own goodness. And she was so overwhelmed and in love with her own goodness that she continued poisoning these squat, chubby dogs until they melted like ice cream cones and slithered down the edge of the living room couch to join all those white hairs they'd shed on her black carpet.

Lucille newman was paul's aunt, the wife of arthur newman sr.'s brother, joe

Both of the Newman boys, Paul and Arthur Jr., must accept that their mother and father were both unwell. Sick in the sense that they had never known true serenity and were drowning.

Given her temper, Art Sr. might have done something quite crazy if he sought to divorce Trees. She was a lonely person, and some of her actions were simply cruel.

I'm not sure what type of life Art Sr. would have had if he'd married someone else; there was a huge attraction there. And he represented a sense of security to Tress. I'm not sure if she had genuine feelings for him. But she couldn't possibly have loved anything other than the blind, obese dog she fed the sweets to.

One way their marriage may have influenced my father was that he became a secret drinker, an alcoholic. I'd always assumed that cancer was the cause of my father's death in 1950. But it wasn't until recently that we analysed the autopsy results and determined that alcohol's effects on his pancreas were a major contributing factor to his untimely death at the age of fifty-six.

The regimen was as follows: Every evening at 5:30 p.m., the Newman-Stern store would close. My father would walk from there to the Terminal Tower in downtown Cleveland in exactly twelve minutes to catch the rapid-transit train to Shaker Heights. That would give him seven minutes to pop into Fred Harvey's, the bar where all the business people went after work, and swallow two double bourbons with water chasers. He'd race for his train, and when he arrived home, he'd go straight upstairs to his closet, where he kept a bourbon bottle, and pour himself another double.

Babette Newman was one of Arthur Newman sr. 's sister-in-law; she married his brother aaron. Stewart Stern was a highly regarded screenwriter and he was one of Paul Newman's closest friends.

Lucille newman: Tress told me Arthur would do things like this: Let's say it was a holiday, and the children were there, of course, and they were dressed for the occasion and she had prepared a nice dinner, set the table pretty and everything, and he'd go upstairs and put on the dirtiest old rotten clothes he could find and come down to the table looking a wreck.

Babette Newman: Just a sad, sad thing. You want to cry.

LN: It's terrible.

Stewart stern: But what was he protesting, I wonder? Her perfection? He wanted to dirty it up and make it liveable, do you think?

BN: Well, I know that I never saw Tress without being perfect. Her hair was beautifully-

LN: Right to the last minute of her life, and she was wearing wigs.

BN: He may have been protesting that.

There would be kiosks along the rapid transit route where you could purchase periodicals, candies, bubble gum, and, at one point, 3.2 percent alcohol. The beer was called Fort Pitt, and the label depicted cowboys and Indians. Arthur and I, who were probably eleven and twelve at the time, persuaded our father to purchase us a bottle one Sunday afternoon. We brought it back to the house, and he opened it and toasted us with much fanfare. When I first tasted it, I thought to myself, "God, what ailment is this?" "Who would want to drink something like that?" It was dreadful.

My father was unconcerned. "You desired it. We requested it. You didn't enjoy it. You'd better finish it now."

I downed it and vowed to myself that I would never drink another glass of beer again.

Art and I never saw our father truly inebriated. We knew he'd taken the edge off before supper, and we'd uncover empty liquor bottles hidden in a crawl area near our basement years later. It's no surprise he went downstairs so frequently to check on the furnace. We later discovered piles of hidden cigarette butts. Though Arthur and I were frequently chastised for sneaking cigarettes up in our attic "club," it turns out that our father was regularly smoking his own cigarettes-despite swearing to my mother that he wasn't.

When Paul and Arthur returned to the house for Tress's funeral, they wanted to see if the dent in the wall where they had banged their heads was still there, and if the hole in the third-floor screen where they had shoved their cigarettes for fear of being caught smoking them was still there.

I didn't want successive generations of Newmans performing secret activities in various rooms. If my son, Scott, smoked marijuana, I'd join him. In recent years, I've wondered if the significant difficulties I finally had with alcohol, and Scott's terrible addiction, were partly inherited-bad blood with the Newman men. And I frequently wonder if my father's drinking had anything to do with the difficulty we had speaking.

My strongest memory of my father (which best characterises our relationship) occurred when I was around twelve years old. On a Sunday, my father remarked to me, "Let's go take a walk." I was overjoyed and astounded by the opportunity. We walked for a long time, but I couldn't think of anything to say to him. He also couldn't think of anything to say that would elicit a response from me. We could only manage rhetorical conversations such as "Isn't that a nice tree?" or "Isn't that a nice fire hydrant?" I'd move sideways, half-skipping, staring up at him, and he'd simply nod affirmatively. We didn't exchange a single thought.

Only by asking inquiries do children learn about their parents.

Unless, of course, their mothers and fathers are storytellers and talkers, which I was and am not. My own children were captivated after I started talking to them; but what if you're a nontalker and your children never ask?

I was playing baseball one day when I attempted to catch a fly ball but missed it and landed on top of the ball, severely injuring my ankle. It was just before dinnertime, and I began crawling home. My father passed by, having just returned from the rapid-transit station after work. When I requested him to assist me, he simply said, "Are you kidding?" and walked away. He most likely assumed I was crying. I was rushed to the hospital the next morning when my ankle swelled to the size of a grapefruit. It was discovered to be broken.

There was a general feeling in the house that I couldn't do anything well. My father was indifferent and uninterested, with a sarcastic tone in his remarks. I believe he stopped attempting to motivate me because he felt he had been licked. I didn't try harder to be a well-educated man because I knew I couldn't. I didn't remember reading Schopenhauer in school, and I don't remember what I didn't comprehend. Years later, when Joanne and I were close friends with Gore Vidal, it was difficult for me to be around a man who could speak intelligently about so many things: American writers, Greeks, Romans, and French playwrights, while I was ignorant. I've realised I have a condition that makes it tough for me to listen, hear people, read faster than I can talk, and even memorise. Whatever the case, I never excelled academically and never offered my father anything to be proud of.

The only way for me to feel any feeling of success was to work and earn money. It could have been the single thing I accomplished that genuinely satisfied my father, proving to him that I could be a self-starter capable of finding work on my own. I guess I also had a burning yearning to be independent, to move away from the feeling that I was always being looked for at home. And we were always taken care of-I don't recall my brother and I ever having to clean up after ourselves. I certainly put forth a lot of effort. I was delivering flowers and dry cleaning, carrying pickle barrels and Coca-Cola boxes up and down the stairs for the delicatessen, and even working as a Fuller Brush man for a while. I applied when I was thirteen, and I became an undersized little towhead dragging about this suitcase full of samples that weighed more than and took up the same amount of space as me.

I did have a perfect route in mind, in a working-class neighbourhood off Kinsman Road. My mother would pick me up after school, drop me off with my gear, and then pick me up three hours later. Kinsman was a working-class neighbourhood, and everyone wanted what I was selling: garage brooms, hairbrushes, toothbrushes, whisk brooms-sixty different sorts, high quality, and much less expensive than they'd cost in a store. I didn't have much of a pitch, but I didn't have to walk far from home to house and ended up making around $40 every week.

I remember ringing a doorbell at one place and this extremely good-looking young woman, perhaps twenty-four, answering the door wearing only a slip with her breasts virtually spilling out; she appeared slightly drunk and degenerate to me. "Come on in, little boy," she said, and I immediately realised this was exceedingly unusual and had nothing to do with Fuller Brushes. I bolted, pulling my bag flat on its side, my samples pouring out behind me as I went, quickly assessing my chances of surviving this lady.

The job I had that had the biggest influence on me was delivering newspapers. I was an excellent bike rider, and my paper route was close to my house. There were these massive houses on Shaker Heights Boulevard that would sell for millions of dollars now. All the gorgeous women in their summer dresses, patrician elegance, and ease of grace and manner reminded me of F. Scott Fitzgerald and The Great Gatsby. I developed a strong desire to be wealthy. I'm talking about filthy rich. I acquired it because I saw all these lovely folks I was delivering papers to. And it felt so far away, just out of sight, from anything I could possibly grasp for.

Arthur Newman Jr.

Paul developed drive, energy, and ingenuity as a result of his desire to pull himself out of his circumstances by his bootstraps. Maybe everything he remembers from his childhood and his mother's controlling behaviour planted the roots for all of his drive, energy, and guts. What happens when he develops this self-starting ability? He achieves success.

Art and I had a buddy, Dick Goss, whose family was extremely wealthy-we'd always heard that the father, Colonel Goss, had made a fortune designing chemical-warfare weapons during World War I. Aside from their Shaker Heights home, they also had a plantation in the south and a summer residence in the north. I was strolling through their library one day after school when I noticed their new Christmas tree, which was decked out with lights and five- and ten-dollar bills. When Mrs. Goss, a dignified-looking woman reading in the corner, noticed me, she said, "Good afternoon, Paul." And that's when I said, "Mrs. Goss, excuse me, but could you please explain to me why your Christmas tree has all these five- and ten-dollar bills on it?"

And this was her exact response: "It's to show Dick that money does not grow on trees-it's planted there". It made an impression on me.

Stewart Stern

What would cause the children in such a household to bang their heads on the wall?

Tress was overwhelmingly proud of him, proud of his beauty, and dressed him up like another part of her house, but she would suddenly, for no reason Paul could think of, attack him savagely with a hairbrush then immediately smother him with love. He'd have no idea who she was or who she thought he was. How did he manage to survive?

Paul has informed me that he feels anaesthetised so frequently that he blacks out most of his youth and doesn't remember much of it. What he's been looking for is a solution to the enigma of his being-why he has such a distance from his own emotions that he could feel very little until recently. A bit sad, a little happy-but he could never feel completely satisfied with either.

Jewell Fetzco was a sister of paul's mother, tress.

Tress had married a plumber named Elmer before meeting Art Sr. He was immensely envious of her; if she simply looked at someone, hell would break loose. He brutally beat her. When I went to see her one Sunday, her face was so damaged that I didn't know it was her. "Tress, what happened?" I inquired. She said nothing but, "Well, I just had some trouble."

Elmer was a handsome devil with dark hair, a moustache, and a good build. However, he was as cruel as the dickens. My sister Mae and I warned her that she was going to be killed and that she needed to divorce. She was ashamed about the whole incident, but she agreed to accompany us to court so a judge and an attorney could see what she looked like all beaten. She moved in with Mae for around six months while her divorce was processed; when she returned home one afternoon, everything she owned, including her furniture, had been taken, save for a mattress to sleep on. She yelled.

We took her back to her attorney the next day, and he obtained an order requiring Elmer to return everything. The divorce was finalised not long after.

Tress fell madly in love with Arthur the moment she met him. It didn't matter to her that he was Jewish; she didn't care if his or her family liked it or not. Arthur, I believe, was also in love with her. Tress declared, "I'll get him." That she did.

Babette Newman

Before meeting Tress, Arthur was going out with a lovely woman with whom he was madly in love. He married Tress on the rebound after she rejected him. Tress resembled the woman who had turned him down.

Jewell Fetzco

Tress was living alone in an apartment at the time Arthur Jr. was born. I had no idea why our mother had sent me to stay with her. "Where is Arthur?" Tress was the one I asked. "Why do I have to be here with you all the time?"

I was a stupid kid. Then, after she began to show, she didn't bring it up again. You didn't bring it up. When she finally told me she was pregnant, she explained that Arthur's family did not accept her, which is why he refused to come live with her. All I remember is that she sobbed a lot.

Lucille Newman

Tress was a beautiful, clever, and accomplished woman. But her sense of values was not your average set of values-she would rather sacrifice people than her house or any part of it. Tress had to leave home quite early, and she had always desired the security of a house. She was always so concerned about their home's security that she would not even let someone in to clean, hang wallpaper, or paint. Even after she sold the house many years later, she kept the chandelier and replaced it with another because it was a part of her. She once gave me six salad bowls as a gift. A few days later, she called and said, "You really don't need six, do you?" She returned four of them.

Scott Newman, when he was a child, locked himself in one of the upstairs restrooms and couldn't get out. Tress would not allow Paul to break down the door. To get Scott out, he had to phone the fire department and have them enter through the bathroom window.

CHAPTER II

I remember a lot more about elementary and junior high school than I do about high school. How the locations appeared. The lecture halls and auditoriums. How it felt to walk home. I felt very much a part of those schools and the community that surrounded them. I felt welcomed and included.

I rode my bike well and dangerously, which was fairly daring. We'd go along the rapid-transit rails to where the streetcars stopped, where there were vending machines selling ice cream and soda pop. We also had yo-yo contests, and I was really adept at those.

We'd play hockey in the winter, digging holes in vacant lots to fill with water and freeze; there was also a large pond for hockey or ice skating. On Sundays, we'd take our car to the outskirts of Shaker Heights, the end of civilization, and my father would teach Art and me how to drive our Studebaker. Sometimes we'd go to Akron and get sandwiches at a wonderful barbecue establishment. I recall these times fondly; they were carefree.

Then, around the time I entered adolescence, something in me shut down. I'm not sure what it was, but I started to feel like an outcast. I started to feel like I was on the outside looking in, and I had no idea what I was looking for inside. I became agonisingly shy. I tried to play football, but even though I knew I was fast, everyone else seemed to have grown five times bigger than me, and I couldn't compete.

I was so little that I had to receive special permission from my principal to play on the ninth-grade team; at fourteen, I weighed less than a hundred pounds. I felt like a complete freak. Because I was so short, I didn't know how to interact with girls; they thought I was a joke, a cheerful clown. I was a lightweight-a label that applied to every aspect of my existence.

I began to notice that certain other people were truly original, instinctive at whatever they did, and everyone could tell. Everyone could tell the difference between a natural football player and one who had to work hard to achieve their goals. Everyone could tell the difference between great lovers-excellent because they were instinctive-and those who studied love. Some people were simply themselves, while the remainder were academics.

I wasn't born to be anything. I wasn't a romantic. I wasn't a sportsperson. I wasn't even a student. I wasn't in charge. I measured things by what I wasn't rather than what I was. I had the impression that there was something missing in me that I couldn't bridge, didn't understand, and couldn't conceive. It wasn't sinking in with me. I didn't get the message.

So it comes as a big surprise to me when I read accounts today from individuals who knew me growing up and claim they saw me as some swaggering romantic, as a loner too confident to bother with their company. I was simply too bashful to pursue connections with the folks I desired to be friends with. I was scared they'd detect me as a forger and simply slap me on the back and say, "See you around."

I was just interested in girls; they were all I could think about. And I just wasn't very good at them.

Sex was viewed differently in my youth than it is now. Back then, if you accidently left a button on your pants open and someone said, "Hey, your fly is open," you'd be in fits of embarrassment for a month. Talking about sex in the 1930s is like talking about individuals dressed in furs and wielding clubs in the Stone Age. If Playboy magazine existed back then, I would have severed my arm just to get a look. I had to sneak into our library's stack of National Geographics and look through pages that were already softened by use if I wanted to view a photo of a woman's breasts. Either that, or I'll ride my bike down to Hathaway Brown, an all-girls boarding school in Shaker Heights, around twilight and try to catch a sight of some unfortunate girl going naked past the window on her way to the shower. Or go to that new house on Eaton Road where the lady who moved in installed a two-way mirror in her bathroom by accident. From afar, she unwittingly served quite a few prepubescent neighbourhood boys until she and her husband figured out the situation and put up some blinds.

There were no adult films available. There will be no nasty postcards. And no unclean females, which made it difficult to obey my mother's instruction that any sexual intemperance should be exercised solely with ladies of the lower order, not the well-bred Shaker Heights ladies. My mother's lofty beliefs may have stemmed from her realisation that she had once been the woman soiled and stomped on, forced to carry children out of wedlock-and her amazement at now being a member of the upper class herself made her resolve that Art and I must remain unsoiled. The best Arthur and I could accomplish was the old burlesque house on Cleveland's 9th Street. I'm not sure how we got in; I must have looked nine years old; perhaps I hid beneath someone's coat. Anyway, it was completely engrossing. Arthur, on the other hand, ran home and attempted to sterilise himself.

I appear to have gotten the short end of the stick from my first sexual memories. I went into the bushes with Dorothy Frances and her friend when I was around six or seven years old and said, "I'll show you mine if you show me yours." And I showed them mine, but they simply smiled and held their panties, refusing to show me theirs. Later, in junior high, I went on my first hayride and barn dance, and I knew I was about to embark on a major sexual adventure. What I didn't realise was how serious my hay fever was, and I started sneezing just as Mary Jane Phipps was about to relax in the hay and enjoy my advances. I was completely paralyzed. There would be no long kissing because I couldn't breathe through my nose.

Mother fired Ruth, our long-time maid, not long after; I'd heard it was because she'd gotten pregnant by her lover. She was quickly replaced with a seventeen-year-old girl who had finished second in a Cleveland high school beauty pageant. My mother put her in the same room as Art and me. What could be better than being a fourteen-year-old boy with a beautiful seventeen-year-old female around who you could envision banging? I would have been such an eager and nervous student! The pleasures that could have arisen, the dalliances between two and four o'clock when she had a couple of hours off! But I was denied that opportunity. My mother, the harridan, was omniscient and prowling everywhere, and it wasn't long until she spotted me in the girl's room, where we were merely staring at each other provocatively. The next day, the new maid was packed and gone.

Even after I enrolled at Ohio University before being drafted, my losing record persisted. I auditioned for a part in a student musical and was cast (most likely because there were so few other men on campus due to the war). It didn't take long for me to fall for another cast member, a statuesque French beauty who was probably a full head taller than me; I liked dancing with her because I could easily rest my head between her boobs. I believe she was uninterested in me, but I did eventually get an actual date with her. If not getting laid, I had dreams of sliding my lips across her neck. I returned her to the hostel, and as I begged for an invitation up to her room, she rubbed my head and remarked, "I like going out with you because you're so harmless!"

I saw a poll in a prominent magazine in the late 1950s when they asked a lot of women which well-known figure they had sexual dreams about. Whose image were they using while they mistreated themselves? The "winner" was, of course, me. Which is amusing until you realise that if I'd been murdered in my bomber during WWII, if I'd gone down in flames, that would have been the hottest things would have gotten for me-I'd only been laid twice. That is a fact that would have both pleased and irritated my mother. The young girl who took my virginity (which I quickly disposed of) was a lady I'd met in a sketchy part of town. For the fact, my second contact was with a lady of extremely high birth in Jacksonville, Florida, where I would be undergoing part of my naval training. Needless to say, neither of these breakthroughs occurred until I was safely out of my house and on my way to battle the Japanese in the South Pacific.

Religion was also associated with a strong sense of otherness. Being partly Jewish-or even thinking of oneself as Jewish-used to prevent me from sitting at the "A" table, which was essential to me. Nothing in my youth taught me anything about my Jewish background that would have made me proud or informed about it. I simply knew that if you were Jewish, some avenues you might have loved to walk down were closed to you. That harmed both myself and my brother greatly. And I believe there was a time in my life when I tried to make amends.

One method was to use humour to distract from the discomfort. The attacks were launched not just because I was Jewish, but also because I was so small. (After being punched and sat on a few times, you learn how to escape punishment.) For fun, I began doing Yiddish voices, volunteering to do an impersonation of Schlepperman, a popular recurring character on Jack Benny's radio show, played by Sam Hearn with a thick Yiddish accent.

When I was about fifteen, I became aware of exclusion. I was applying to a popular high school fraternity when Arthur warned me, "I wouldn't expect much." You'll be rejected because you're half Jewish." And I said to myself, "No, that could never possibly be true." But then my friend Roger returned from his frat meeting and broke the bad news to me: "God," he said, "I'm really sorry, but there are things in our bylaws that say we can't have Jewish brothers."

I'm ashamed that I was insecure enough to be deceitful, or at the very least not completely honest, on my original Kenyon College application following my service in the Navy. My religion was requested on the application. I didn't simply type "Preference: None" or "Half Catholic, Half Jewish." I wrote in the language of my mother's adopted faith, claiming to be a Christian Scientist. Aside from that, I never hid my past from anyone; no one had to pry it out of me, and I never denied it.

It's probably not a coincidence that the only violent brawl I got into during WWII contained an anti-Semitic remark. On my route to the Pacific theatre, I was stationed in Hawaii. There was a beer garden for the sailors, but you couldn't carry the beer away with you. I devised a plan to smuggle the bottles out by donning a denim jacket and concealing four or five brews inside my belt. The plan was to sneak over a back wall, then return to your barracks with the contraband. One of the sailors stood up from his bunk and told me I owed him a beer. "For what?" I responded. "You kike, you owe me a beer." I charged him, and a huge brawl ensued. Though I wasn't much of a puncher, I had wrestled at Ohio University and had an exceptional sense of balance that allowed me to throw down an opponent, jump on top of him in midair, and fall on him. When I fell on him, his arm was beneath his hip and he tore everything out of his elbow. He could barely move one hand when he got up from the floor. The fight ended, and no one troubled me again.

Years later, as my acting career took off, I was given the option to pass, to change my identity and become a Tony Curtis (born Bernard Schwartz) or Kirk Douglas (called Issur Danielovich). Broadway and Hollywood suggested I become Buck Something-or-Other, a truly WASPy identity; and I could have gotten rid of my Jewish heritage entirely, just erasing the source of my unease. But keeping my real name, insisting on it as a badge, was more of a struggle to me.

In 1953, the legendary, merciless producer Sam Spiegel, who went by the alias S. P. Eagle for nearly two decades, was briefly considering me for the role of Terry Malloy in On the Waterfront; he wanted me to remove "Paul Newman." "What exactly do you want me to change it to?" I inquired. "S. P. Ewman?"

Unlike some of his family, my father was never a practising Jew. Nonetheless, he kept two seats at our local synagogue, which he paid for year after year. My mother told him one weekend, "I'd like to go over to that synagogue, see what it's like there." And so it went: the husband and the wife, whom he frequently took out late on Saturday evenings so she wouldn't have the stamina to get up in time for her Christian Science service on Sunday morning. The only difficulty was that when they entered the synagogue, my father's seats were already taken. So my father went straight to the business office, where he was informed that they had actually sold his seats twice; what harm could it do since he never attended services? After some back-and-forth, my father agreed to keep those seats for the rest of his life in order for him and my mother, the Gentile, to be buried side by side in the Jewish cemetery run by the synagogue. And so it was.

My father wore no visible Jewish symbols other than the pew he rented. We celebrated Christmas with carolling and a huge pile of nicely wrapped gifts beneath an impressive tree (which, to my sorrow, my mother insisted on purchasing, and she embraced a metallic one with the dreadful artificiality that implied). My father didn't have a menorah in our house, despite receiving a daily edition of Cleveland's Jewish newspaper. Nonetheless, he was far from oblivious to the prejudices that Jews faced over the world.

Though we rarely took family vacations, we did take a summer trip to Maine one year. Despite the fact that we were in the midst of the Great Depression, my father insisted on us travelling in elegance, and he reserved a cabin at the Black Point Inn on Prouts Neck. It was grand, on the sea, surrounded by blueberry plants, and unmistakably stuffy, ritzy, and very Gentile-a point not missed on my father, who registered us under an assumed, very non-Jewish name. To be honest, I believe they only let us check in because we were driving a nice Studebaker Commander.

Bush Keeler was a close childhood friend of Paul's.

Shaker Heights had a heavy Jewish stigma. My mother, I'm sure, had reservations about me seeing a lot of Paul since he was Jewish. She wasn't pleased with our company. Her actual self liked Paul, but her socially conditioned self was ambivalent. She just wanted me to be a part of that dreaded private-school crowd. Paul didn't appear Jewish at all, but he paid a price and had a difficult life. There used to be a lot of ethnic slurs regarding Jews floating around high school. Paul was a witty individual who could find humour in practically any situation. And that's how he overcame his prejudice. Do you remember the character Schlepperman from the old Jack Benny show? Paul was the expert impersonator, and he had everyone in stitches. I believe he did it to let them know they were hurting him. Someone used to tease him, but he always came back laughing.

Jim Martin was one of Paul's closest friends in shaker heights and through college.

I thought the younger Paul was extremely frivolous. I had the impression he was content and had nothing to hide. Tress, Paul's mother, was an extremely amazing person. After school, she'd usually have a large strawberry cake cooked for us. But I was also concerned that Paul's family appeared depressed. The place was always spotless. We'd have to take off our shoes before entering. The furniture in the living room was always covered in sheets-lamps, sofas, everything. It didn't appear like anyone lived there.

CHAPTER III

My one and only repeating nightmare is merely sound, and it has never left me. It's quite impressionistic at first, just a sense of clouds with a sense of ease about them. And suddenly it's as if these clouds are accompanied by an unidentifiable roar. Rustling leaves, perhaps, or the sound of water, but always closer and closer. There's a lot of roiling going on, nothing recognizable, until it can't get any closer or any louder. But it gets closer and louder and closer and louder and closer and louder and closer and louder. It's wind, sea, and sound, but it's never identified. I've had this nightmare since I can remember. Never more detailed, yet somehow foreboding. I had never flown before, and I had no idea what it was like to be on an aeroplane during a rainstorm when that nightmare began. Something similar to that menace exists in my dream. It frightens me.

***

On December 7, 1941, my father went for a Sunday stroll and returned to our house via the side entrance. He was as pale as a sheet and informed us that the Japanese had just bombed Pearl Harbor. For all that it meant to me, he might have stated Mickey and Minnie Mouse had just given birth to four puppies. I had no notion where Pearl Harbor was located. I had no idea what a war was or what it entailed. I had no idea what cancer was. These were the years of my most superficial illiteracy. I was only living in my brain. I was preoccupied with imagining a thrilling world in which I was the White Knight who defeated all adversaries, a world in which I stood seven and a half feet tall and only accomplished essential things.

***

I often tell people - and I know it's been written about - that I was kicked out of the Navy's pilot-training program after it was revealed that I was colorblind. But it's a little more involved than that; in retrospect, it was a collection of issues rather than just my colour blindness. I couldn't perform the mathematical tasks required of a pilot. I'm not very good at hard science. It does not pass through. This is not to say I am unwilling to learn it, but the more I focus on how to grasp something rather than actually understanding it, the more we appear to be in trouble. Physics, trigonometry, and chemistry were all too difficult for me. I became discouraged and gave up.

When the conflict broke out, I hadn't even graduated high school. And, as usual, after graduation in June 1942, when I was still seventeen, I had no concrete idea for what I intended to accomplish. But I was aware that if you didn't further your education, you'd be drafted as soon as you turned 18 and end up swabbing decks on a battleship. This was a major reason I enrolled at Ohio University-going to college would allow me to make some decisions for myself, at least in terms of the military. So, when I started college at Ohio University in Athens, I also enlisted, knowing that my official call to duty would be no earlier than my eighteenth birthday, on January 26 (and probably later); I took the written aptitude exams and applied for pilot training.

To my astonishment, I was pulled from school and driven to Detroit for a physical shortly after my birthday. And I was astonished since I failed the exam because the medical examiners revealed I was colorblind. (I should have gotten a heads-up a few months ago when my brother, Arthur, emailed me that he'd been turned down for pilot training because-guess what?-the doctors discovered he was colorblind.)

So I had the option of continuing with my officer enlistment procedures or withdrawing and returning to Ohio U to wait for my draft number to be called. But, I wondered, for what purpose? I'd enjoyed the acting classes I'd taken during my first semester, but Ohio U was nothing but beer and dating. The only thing that set me apart was that I was a fantastic chug-a-lugger. And, despite the fact that it was taking an eternity for my Navy paperwork to be reprocessed and officially removing me from the pilot program, I was still sent to deck officers' training school, which was held on the Yale University campus. I was billeted in a facility that was essentially an old extension to the best dormitory there by chance. I had a large living room with a bedroom off to the side, as well as a wood-burning fireplace. If I'd been a successful student in New Haven, my colour blindness would have gone unnoticed; nevertheless, I was soon sent from university and back to square one to attend enlisted men's boot camp, or basic training, in Newport, Rhode Island.

Hundreds of aspiring sailors resided in my barracks, and like me, they were allocated to a hammock rather than a bunk bed-I didn't get a good night's sleep for four months. We were awakened at four thirty or five every morning-and it was cold. The first order of business was callisthenics, followed by a couple of kilometres of running. These were difficult days for me because I was out of shape and smoking cigarettes.

I was obliged to have another physical while in Newport. One of the corpsmen in charge of the exams was a guy I met at Yale; he'd been kicked out of medical school there and wound up in my boot camp as a pharmacist's mate, third class. And when he gave me the colour-chart test, I discovered that I was no longer colorblind.

That meant I could now apply for the Naval Air Corps as an enlisted man. No, I probably couldn't be a pilot, but I applied for and was accepted for training as an aviation radioman. So I was assigned to radio school in Jacksonville, where I completed the course and volunteered to fly torpedo bomber planes. General Motors produced thousands of these TPM Avenger bombers, which were slow, lumbering, single-propeller aircraft with only three-man crews—a pilot, a machine gunner in a "bubble" directly above the cockpit, and a radioman/gunner in a turret under the plane's belly. The top speed was barely around 150 miles per hour. The primary function of the TPM was to detect enemy submarines and torpedo them from the air. We'd see a sub, lock the gyroscopic aiming mechanism on it, then dive down to between six and fifteen feet over the water and maintain a steady position before firing. As a result, the TPMs became sitting ducks for enemy planes, ideal for target practice.

My next visit was Miami for gunnery classes (my instructor was Robert Stack), and to be honest, I wasn't a particularly skilled machine gunner. Then it was headed to Southern California's Oxnard Air Base, and then to Pearl Harbor as part of a squadron of six TPMs. During my Florida training, I became friends with two sailors: Milt Dance, whom we called Danny and who came from the Maryland shore, and Tommy Brady, a tough little guy from Boston. We were initially drawn together because we were all around the same size; we were all good-time Charlies who learned we liked to laugh a lot. When we were asked for our preferred assignments, Danny and I both requested torpedo-bomber service, whereas Brady ended up on a dive-bomber squad.

Brady was killed a few days later on his first drill fly off the Florida coast when his plane's wing was struck by another dive bomber's wing and crashed in midair. I recall being taken aback by the news, but I didn't immediately associate it with myself. I don't even remember feeling nervous about going on an airline after that. There must have been a strange, magnificent sensation of immortality back then. As well as my own evolving form of emotional anaesthesia. It never occurred to me that there was a chance we wouldn't survive.

Milton Dance was a torpedo plane crewmate of Paul's throughout wwii.

When we were training for gunnery, they flew a towed sleeve behind a plane, and you had to hit it with your anti-aircraft gun. Each sailor was given a belt of coloured ammunition, so when you shot through the sleeve, it was easy to determine whose bullets hit and went through.

Paul couldn't hit beans or that towed sleeve with the turret gun to qualify as our plane's gunner. However, someone on another crew had hit it, firing fifty rounds with red casings through that sleeve. "Paul was shooting those red ones, that's him!" We told the Navy trainers when we landed.

***

We remained in Hawaii while our squadron awaited orders to be assigned to a battleship. Every morning, I'd report to the flight shack, a little wooden structure next to one of the hangars. We had to take off for flight drills on occasion, but we mostly sat around all day, playing Hearts and drinking a little beer (after five o'clock, of course). I did spend a lot of my free time reading a lot, mostly philosophy by Spinoza and Nietzsche; I was trying to gain an education, and I'm sure I was also trying to impress people. There were also a slew of letters from my family to sort through; I seemed to be getting more mail than anyone else in our flying party. Arthur would write to me from his base in England on a regular basis, and my father corresponded with me almost every day I was in the Army. My father's letters were fairly unemotional, often focusing on keeping me informed about what was going on at Newman-Stern.

And my comments were far from candid. I told lies to my brother, my mother, and my father. Personal deceptions at their worst. I can't think of anything true that came from my letters except "I stood watch last night." But there wasn't a single astute perception in any of them, which is what I despise the most about myself.

To be honest, I was far more interested in receiving letters from a handful of females I'd abandoned. Joan Gloeckler is the one I remember best. She had a fantastic physique and was incredibly attractive; we were in the same class at Shaker Heights High. I don't think it was anything consistent, but there was a sense that we were suddenly romantic shortly before I left for the war. I wouldn't call it a heated love affair; perhaps it was just wishful thinking, but having someone back home you felt was your girlfriend was soothing. While I was in the Navy, she wrote to me for a long time. However, about a year before the war ended, she sent me another letter in which she stated that she had found another guy; I was gone. It hurt my heart; I'm not sure why, because it was never serious.

A group of us would occasionally receive a pass and travel to a location just north of Barbers Point, about sixty miles from Honolulu. There was an incredible beach there with really nice sand and pleasantly warm water. You'd spend a couple of hours sprinting into these five- or six-foot waves that would crash against an angled falloff point close to the coast, and you'd get bowled over teakettle with no movement or restriction. You'd be washed up on the beach like a frog again and again. Our entire squadron would travel there, and the Hawaiians would host a luau for us, cooking a whole pig outside.

On several days, Danny and I would fly some anti submarine exercises, strafing targets towed by target planes, or dropping depth charges. Then we'd go back to the barracks and hang out with the other crews; it was utter boredom.

The most exciting-and terrifying-thing that happened to me was when Danny and I agreed to take part in a little "experiment."

The Navy was anxious that our planes assaulting the Japanese mainland might be shot down by coastal artillery and crash into Tokyo Bay. What needed to be tested was a means for Allied submarines to save survivors from downed planes' life rafts. The plan was for our subs to capture the lifeboats and haul them into deeper water unobserved by the Japanese, where the airmen could be hoisted on board-all hands safely out of range of the Japanese solid shore weapons.

Danny and I assumed it would be a minor distraction. So we set out for a staging spot, where our test raft launch had to be cancelled due to sharks in the sea. So we were transported to a different location, where each of us was placed in a one-man raft tied together by a rope and then abandoned together in the Pacific Ocean to await our underwater voyage back home.

We'd brought a handful of condoms with us, which we used to keep our keys, cigarettes, and cookies dry. We released green-dye markers around us as directed to increase our visibility to our planes. Dive bombers would be dispatched to locate us and transmit our location to surrounding submarines. It was a lot of fun. At first, yes.

So we sat and waited. And then I waited some more. The sea was rising, the air was getting cold, and we were dressed in sweaters and shorts. We were alone in the ocean, with no sign of any aircraft.

A large amphibious transport boat appeared out of nowhere, unrelated to our experiment but having observed our colour marks. They indicated that they were going our way, but we responded by signalling back. "Go away, go away!" They ignored us and shortly launched a smaller ship that drew alongside our rafts. "Get on board," the commanding officer shouted, but he finally got the point when we answered, "We can't-we're doing a test." I swear the ship's waist gunner was so enraged at us that he unlatched his safety and contemplated pulling the trigger. They lifted off, and we continued to scan the sky for our rescue dive bombers.

They finally appeared late that afternoon. A Navy submarine was a half hour behind them. It was strange to watch a submarine approaching you at sea level; it had about eight feet of periscope targeting us, but when it tried to snag our cable to haul us out of danger, it utterly missed. It could only see us from a certain angle. The sub sailed past us for about 150 feet before realising we weren't linked. We laughed until the sun made another rush at us, caught us, and began to pull. Nobody expected that with our attachment at the top of the rafts, a sub would draw us not just forward but also beneath the surface; we were pulled for almost two miles and held on for dear life. The submarine then began to surface. I had no idea what the hell was going on. It's difficult to put into words how it feels to be on a tiny raft when this massive behemoth starts blowing its tanks and rising out of the sea. The roar was incredible; this was the one time I was truly terrified. Worse, the sub's antenna pierced the bottom of Danny's raft and nearly impaled him in the buttocks.

We were secure, but there is a postscript. The skipper welcomed us aboard his submarine and noted that we were blue.

"God, you guys must be frozen!" he exclaimed.

So we were grateful when the skipper vanished for a bit and reappeared with an ancient and really fine bottle of Canadian rye. He poured a couple of fingers for the three of us, we smashed them down, and then he poured another round.

"Well," the skipper explained, "I'm supposed to ask you some questions about the rescue now." "Please provide me with your names, ranks, and serial numbers."

"Sir, my name is Paul Newman. I'm not a police officer. I don't have a position. "I'm a third-class aviation mate."

"You're an enlisted man?"

"Yes," I said. He then took our whiskey and poured it right back into the bottle.

In my war, alcohol would play an interesting role. Danny and I were assigned to an ensign pilot named Pat Filippi. Pat, like the other officers, would be given a monthly booze allowance. Pat would frequently donate his bottles to Danny and me because he didn't drink.

If we didn't drink it ourselves, we'd sell it to other enlisted men for anywhere from $50 to $100, depending on the going rate that week. I had more than enough money to begin with, because my monthly salary as a third-class mate was $78, plus a 50% bonus for flight duty. The issue was that I was a poor gambler. I'd lose my entire check in an hour of playing poker, shooting craps, and blackjack. So I had to earn it back by playing bridge for money against the pilots and selling the booze Pat gave me. And what did I do with this money? Of course, to purchase beer. If I wasn't able to steal it.

My TPM crew (and our plane) sailed much closer to the battle zone, laying anchor off Guam, just after we were eventually ordered to leave Hawaii. We were all irritated the first night we arrived on the island since there was no beer rationing. But it didn't take long for us to figure out where the beer and liquor stash was kept.

Everything was housed beneath a large supply tent and was guarded by two marine personnel. While the rest of us sneaked under the canvas to where the beer cases were stored, we sent a couple of decoys over to the sentries to ask directions to the infirmary and distract them. We weren't planning on searching through thousands of dollars of wine; we just intended to steal a few for ourselves and sneak back to our bunks. Instead, we all ended up simply sitting under the tent, thankfully back on dry land, and bullshitting each other until we heard taps and the lights went out.

"Let's go," one of my companions offered, while another responded,

"Well, why don't we just wait until things calm down a little bit?" That is exactly what we did. Until we heard gunshots. One of the marine sentries discovered two other soldiers slipping under the tent and shot them both. I'm not sure if they survived or were killed, but they were clearly injured. Needless to say, my crew quickly exited and decided not to attempt that act again.

We'd arrived in Guam on a CVE, which everyone referred to as a "jeep carrier." These were converted troop transporters or freighters that served as our floating home till the war's end. The CVEs resembled small aircraft carriers, complete with a flight deck, but their runways were much, much shorter, making them much frightening. This resulted in numerous white-knuckle landings, especially in inclement weather when the CVE's nose was constantly rising and lowering in the surf.

We had a routine patrol flight one afternoon with a pilot I didn't know who was standing in for Pat. We came in for a landing, and just as we were about to touch down, the deck controller gave us a wave-off, forcing us to climb and circle again. It made me a little anxious because this was generally done only if a plane came in with the runway inaccurately aligned. We began another descent and were again waved off; I was becoming increasingly uneasy, especially as I was in the turret with my back to the cockpit and couldn't see what was going on.

So we circled again, and this time we weren't allowed to land, which made me nervous. This time, however, when he was waved off, our pilot turned to the right of the bridge, which was unheard of since it was extremely dangerous-if you missed your manoeuvre, you'd strike the carrier. We were finally allowed to land the next time we approached, and as soon as we came to a stop, our pilot leaped out of our plane and began ranting aggressively at the sailor who'd been waving us off. We later discovered that there was nothing wrong with our pilot's flying, but that on board our CVE was a photographer from one of the big weekly magazines taking photos of planes touching down on a flattop. He wanted the perfect photograph, and the Navy was only assisting him by providing further material for his photo essay.

We were quite fortunate. When we were still in Hawaii, the six planes in our original TPM group were assigned to report to the USS Bunker Hill, one of the Seventh Fleet's most powerful carriers. But our pilot felt unwell that morning, and we were grounded; we never went there, and we became an unaffiliated plane waiting to be a replacement on one of the other huge ships-an improbable scenario for an unattached aircraft, given that entire squadrons were usually assigned together. Late in the war, two kamikazes carrying 550-pound bombs assaulted the Bunker Hill off the coast of Okinawa. One of the suicide pilots broke into the flight tower and pilot's ready room, igniting massive fires and murdering nearly 400 sailors, including ten of the fifteen crew members from the squadron to which we were assigned.

***

We sailed from Guam to Saipan, where we disembarked after one of the war's bloodiest engagements. Even though our commanders warned us to be on the lookout for Japanese army stragglers invading our camp at night for food, I don't believe it was particularly dangerous by the time we arrived. In reality, eight or ten of us marched into the highlands one day looking for souvenirs-discarded helmets, uniforms, or ammunition belts-but there were no Japanese survivors to be found. The worst part was when we hiked into a thicket and I was assaulted by a swarm of yellow jackets; I believe I was bitten twenty-four times.

The majority of our time was spent on our jeep-carrier ship. Everyone was talking about our impending invasion of Japan, how we were truly preparing for a last assault, and how the possibility for massive losses in that invasion was quite high.

When we learned about the A-bomb and later the capitulation, we were about 75 miles off the Japanese mainland. There was a profound sense of relief that this was all over. Our CVE was ordered back to Pearl Harbor just a few days after Nagasaki. The first thing that sprang to mind was "Here we go again-we'll all get stuck there for another year before we're discharged." However, as we approached Hawaii, new orders were sent that basically ordered, "Keep going." So, without pausing, we drove straight to San Francisco. We docked and were given a two-week leave with instructions to report back in Seattle.

But first, there was some celebrating to do. Some pilots I met on board reserved a large suite at the renowned Mark Hopkins Hotel, and a couple dozen of us sailors stayed for three days. There was no orgy, but things became very wild. The pilots would go downstairs to the Mark Hopkins bar, pick up some gals, and transport them upstairs to the celebration. I recall a lot of flight crew guys going around in their boxer shorts, and the girls thought we were all officers. In the morning, you'd wake up and start drinking beer again. Remember, the war had only been over for about three weeks at the time, and we were all acting poorly.

My five months in Seattle ended up being similarly "productive." I was posted to an aeroplane hangar, where I was forced to perform mechanical tasks for which I was unqualified. That, or assisting with the removal of old generators from Hellcat planes.

I needed money to keep from going bankrupt because I was still losing money gambling. To that purpose, I persuaded guys who were about to be discharged to give me their ID and their booze coupons, which allowed the bearer to buy liquor on the cheap. Joe Beeler, a sailor from Kansas, had received $1,300 from his father to purchase a used car, and he chose a four-door Pontiac. I made a bar out of scrap wood and metal that we stretched over the back seat; I carpeted it and cut holes in the plywood for bottles, glasses, and even an ice chest. There was no other limousine that looked anything like that in 1946.

We primarily employed the Pontiac for three purposes. We'd take a few of the girls we met at the University of Washington up to Mount Rainier on weekends to go skiing. It was an expensive idea, so we ran a car service from the base to the mountains during the week, and we'd take pilots and other officers for a fee. Beeler and I would wax skis, go skiing, and still make it back to the parking lot in time to take our passengers back to town. When we drove to the downtown Seattle dancing halls, which closed at midnight, we did our best job. There were a lot of males around who had picked up girls but now didn't have anywhere to drink. So Beeler and I would drive up and simply stand there with these unlabeled pints and quarts of whiskey. We'd charge them $15 or $25 each, and the money would cover our next week's ski outings with the girls, with enough left over to buy them dinner.

I was honourably discharged in April 1946, returned to Shaker Heights, and enrolled at Kenyon College by June 1. Perhaps the most notable result of my time in the military was that I really shot up. I was just five feet five inches tall when I walked in. I was at least five inches taller when I left.

***

For all the impact the war had on me, it was probably the same as being in a touring company of Shakespeare's The Taming of the Shrew passing through Schenectady, Poughkeepsie, and upstate New York. There was no sense of surprise. There is no sense of survival. There was little sense of danger, and much less of maturation or maturation as a result of it. That's all. It was like taking a shower.

CHAPTER IV

Having not been shot down in the Pacific, the really stupid error I made after the war was enrolling at a non-coed school like Kenyon College. I assumed I desired a decent education more than women did. I was a rake, and having women on campus, as I discovered at Ohio University, may cause a diversion in my attention; going coed would be disastrous for me. I could truly focus and concentrate in an all-male school. The problem was that without women, women became the fixation. You spent every waking hour trying to figure out how to acquire yourself as a Gambier, Ohio, town girl. So, rather than having girls on campus and revelling in their company, being able to pick and choose, their absence became the focus.

I had also overlooked Kenyon College's reputation as a party school.

I was sent off by my parents on a Sunday afternoon in June at three o'clock when I became distracted by a beer keg. I was exhausted by six o'clock. That's how long it took me to make friends with the wrong people at Kenyon. So much for self-control. I had no real education when I left Kenyon, but I did own the school's beer-chugalug record. My yearbook photo was captioned, "Prone to getting out of hand on long tiring evenings."

Regrettably, I was not a student of anything. I began by declaring myself an economics major. Perhaps I'd been fantasising about working for my father at Newman-Stern (I even included it on my Kenyon application). I liked the store, and I was a competent salesman, but the prospect of working there bored me. And while I went through my economics subjects, even accounting, I changed my major to political science. To tell you the truth, being on the college football team, boosted by the increased stature I'd gained in the Navy, was what I most loved.

Of course, my plans had to change when I got into disciplinary trouble. This is how it happened, and it all had to do with attending an all-male institution.

Mount Vernon, Ohio, about ten miles east of Kenyon, is where many of us would congregate. There was a club there called the Bluebird Club, which featured live dancing bands or popular canned music on occasion. On weekends, it was the place to go to meet single women in town. And on this particular night, several members of the football squad decided to go together.

The local town boys were really hostile toward us. The townies were our age, but they weren't in school, and many of them worked with their hands for a living. We were the outsider college students, so the hostility was inevitable. It was not uncommon for battles to erupt. What triggered things was that we Kenyon guys were constantly attempting to steal their girlfriends. When the townies returned from the restroom, we'd be dancing with their dates.

Typically, these bouts were more like shoving matches than anything else. Perhaps some black eyes or bloody noses. Nobody ever kicked anyone on the ground, and no one ever hid anything in their pockets. Indeed, in the days following these usual altercations, you might be strolling down the street and encounter one of the townies you fought walking across the street. You'd wave at each other and say, "I'm going to get you next week," to which the other kid would respond, "I'm around," and that was the end of it.

One night, however, things may have gone a bit too far; there had been more of an actual brawl, but it had swiftly died down. However, the club's bartender phoned the cops, and two plainclothesmen entered through the door. Bert Forman, our quarterback, decked one of them before they could get their badges. "Come and get me!" Bert yelled as he walked out into the middle of the dance floor. Bert says, "I'm right here, where do you want me to go?" when one of the cops flashes his badge.

"Who started all of it?" the second plainclothesman asks the bartender. Then the bartender pointed to three or four of our guys, who were immediately marched outside and loaded into police cars. As they were being transported away, one of the guys handed me his keys and said, "Bring my car into town."

So, 45 minutes later, I drove his car to the police station, found the sergeant, and told him, "One of the guys you've got in the slammer asked me to drop his keys off." The sergeant responds, "Let me see your knuckles." And, of course, my knuckles were bloodied from the battle. Before I knew it, the sergeant had stated, "Well, you're in, too," and they had thrown me in with the rest of our comrades.

When I peeked out the bars, I saw the entire courtyard next to the station house packed with Kenyon students who had come out to support us. Someone had gotten a keg of beer, and everyone was sitting on the ground singing old college songs until the authorities dispersed them around three a.m. The whole thing had a terrific sense of humour about it.

The story broke the next day in newspapers across the country, including the Cleveland Plain Dealer-Kenyon's football squad was in hot water. My name was among those jailed, and when my father saw the article, he regarded it as confirmation that I was screwing up, which I was. Three or four students were immediately expelled from Kenyon, and another three or four, including myself, were placed on probation. I was also thrown off the football team for good measure.

With all of this free time on my hands, I walked down to the speech department and auditioned for a play. I had planned to audition for the theatre.

It all made sense. I had done some drama at Ohio University and enjoyed it. Plays were less difficult for me than ordinary classes; I had always struggled with studying from books. One of the reasons was that I had never been taught how to study. I still believe I have a learning handicap, and I still don't read correctly. In fact, I still have trouble remembering scripts.

I'd actually started onstage when I was in elementary school, when we put up a play about Robin Hood, and I played the court jester. I yodelled after singing a song about Robin Hood's bow and arrow that my uncle Joe (who, in addition to being my father's business partner, was a published author of light verse and even the lyricist of the song "Black Cross," recorded by both Lord Buckley and Bob Dylan) had written for me: "Robin Hood he saw a flea / And knocked the fuzz right off its knee / In merry England isle-o" (Before my testicles descended, I was an excellent yodeler. I yodelled until I was 38 years old, waiting and hoping. Well, not that long, but my body did mature slowly—later sprouting hair, later growing taller, later developing testicles. A close friend who was well-versed in psychoanalytic theory once stated that I had subconsciously created the delay in my testicular descent in order to prolong my mother's care for me. "Boy," I said to myself, "that would be one incredible act of will!")

Some people commented, "Isn't he cute?" My mother decided to get me into the theatre regardless of what I wanted to do after a few more stage turns. My mother despised football and did not want me to participate in a game that was intrinsically harmful. When I went to football practice, she was continually fluttering around attempting to put on my eyelashes and correct my lipstick.

My mother wanted me to sing, dance, or do something artistic like become an actor. So Mom took me to the Cleveland Play House, where the great K. Elmo Lowe, an Uncle Joe's buddy, was the creative director. The PlayHouse was a well-known regional theatre that also had a highly recognized children's program called the Curtain Pullers, to which I was admitted. One of the plays we performed was a children's rendition of St. George and the Dragon, in which I played St. George at the age of nine. I didn't kill the dragon, but I did sprinkle salt on its tail, place my foot on its breast, and make a ferocious gesture with my wooden sword. The poor dragon went into a dreadful writhing fit. It even led to my first professional stage photograph. We conducted a few successful shows, and most of the parents came to see us.

***

We would put on between eight and ten productions a year at the Hill Theater at Kenyon. Jim Michael, my instructor, director, and eventually good friend, gave me a lot of confidence by constantly casting me. Did I arrive at that point of comprehension or perception that someone instils in you, plugs you in, and all of a sudden the light turns on? That was not the case. I never had the impression that whatever I did on stage was remarkable or even exciting. It could have been workmanlike or good, but I was a very inexperienced performer. I was a youngster with an appealing exterior, a lot of energy, and a lot of personality. But did I have a natural talent for Shakespeare or naturalistic roles? My theatrical work at Kenyon was simply an average college production; it would have been recognized as the result of a university and a lot of phonetics lessons.

Nothing out of the ordinary was going on in my thinking. "Couldn't you read the signals that people thought you were really something?" everyone asks, shaking their heads. To which I respond, "No."

Consider someone whose experience with practically everything has been average, and who then discovers something that is at least the best of whatever it is that they can do-it isn't fantastic, and it isn't even all that fulfilling, but it is their best. They are aware that they would not make good mechanics, football coaches, or teachers of history or algebra. They could still sell bowling balls if they wanted to, but they don't. So the next best thing they can do is to be linked to the theatre in some way. And, once again, it's not a triumph, but it's the best they can do.

I can't even bring myself to look at the work I accomplished early in my career. That doesn't make me a horrible person, and it doesn't mean I had unrealistic goals. And while that may not be acceptable to you, it is acceptable to me. I simply get so irritated when everyone imposes their standards, assessments, and recollections of what they worked on, what they did, and they assume that's how it happened for me as well.

I never liked acting, and I never liked going out there and doing it. All of the preliminary work-the detail, the observation, the fitting things together-was enjoyable. Every now and then, I'd do a scenario that would come together in an unexpected way, and I'd be amazed. But that was only a small portion of the time I spent doing it.

It's definitely one of the reasons I drank so much. The energy, risk, and joy of performing were magnified by a factor of eighty. I wouldn't have had to go out and be blasted if I had just gotten it from performing.

But I'm already getting ahead of myself.

***

The Front Page was my first major role, and I played the fast-talking, wiseass tabloid editor Hildy Johnson. I don't remember much about our show, but it was certainly warmly received by the audience, and Jim Michael came to believe I had a natural talent for comedy roles. I played everything from Captain Shotover in George Bernard Shaw's Heartbreak House (in which I was a last-minute replacement for another actor and had to learn the script in ten days-not a memory I'm proud of) to Lord Fancourt Babberley in the Victorian farce Charley's Aunt to R.U.R. in Shakespeare's Taming of the Shrew.

I know some folks in the theatre department were taken aback by some of the stage stuff I performed with Katherina in The Taming of the Shrew, especially when I seized her, pushed her to the ground, and straddled her. They thought it was brave even to try it unprompted in rehearsal. But I never felt it was a significant advancement. "Would you like my tongue in your ass, Kate?" Petruchio practically says. When they come together, it's a fairly raunchy scenario. All you have to do is go back and examine the lines.

It reminds me of the reaction to R.U.R. Lots of compliments, but when I think back on it, my attack was actually just very oratory. It was completely out of step with what actors were doing in New York at the time. (When I finally arrived in New York and read for my first stage play with Anne Jackson, she just glanced at me and said, "Don't work so hard. "Do not act."

Performing in Jean Anouilh's Antigone was especially noteworthy since it gave me one of the worst attacks of giggles I've ever had. I played the First Guard, which is a really significant job; he needs to keep an eye on the doomed princess, Antigone, and then report to King Creon the news that "the sergeant found the shovel," which was crucial evidence that Antigone herself had illegally attempted to inter her brother's corpse. For some reason, I thought it was hilarious that someone would think discovering a shovel improved their life, and the line, "The sergeant found the shovel," just made me giggle. And every time I entered the room during rehearsal to say the line, I burst out laughing. The cast became enraged, and no one was able to assist me. The crew took a break, but we had to labour until three a.m. before I could enter stage left and say "The sergeant found the shovel" with a straight face.

It reminds me of a similar scene when we were filming Butch Cassidy and the Sundance Kid years later. Butch puts on a brave front and tries to boost Sundance's drooping morale when Sundance and I step off the train in Bolivia and there's nothing but hovels and pigsties. I just look at Redford and think, "It's hard to believe that just fifty years ago, there was absolutely nothing here." It was a beautiful line, hysterical, and it just shattered my heart. The vintage train we were on had to be backed up for a retake, but as soon as the cameras started rolling again, I burst out laughing. That train continued backing up, and the director, George Roy Hill, attempted everything-long shots, medium shots, whatever-but he eventually called a wrap in surrender. The sentence was never used in the film, and I'm still seeking for a spot to use it.

Anyway, no matter how much attention I received for my onstage work at Kenyon, I never considered my performances to be true achievements; they were simply something I did, nothing more essential than someone studying hard and achieving an A in political science. I was doing the same thing as everyone else in class, on the tennis or football teams. I didn't give it any glitz or celebrity status, nothing like that.

I don't recall the success of those plays; I simply recall the work that went into them. I remember being there, being onstage, the rehearsals, constructing the sets more than anything else about school. And now I recognize that the most significant event in my undergraduate life was entrepreneurial rather than theatrical: it was my laundry business.

Newman's Laundry began with little, but it had ingenuity and addressed things in a revolutionary manner. Despite the fact that many people anticipated disaster and catastrophic consequences for me, it proved to be practically bulletproof and became the greatest triumph of my school days.

Imagine Main Street in Gambier as a nineteenth-century collection of storefronts, a barbershop, and a few little food stores, each about twelve feet across and forty feet deep, like railroad flats. I noticed one space was empty and thought it would be ideal for a laundry collecting service if I could just persuade the Kenyon students to use it. And I figured the only thing that might motivate students would be free beer: bring in your clothing, and we'll give you a beer.

I approached Newark, Ohio's venerable Licking Laundry Company and asked if they'd negotiate a deal with me. They informed me that if I could make $200 per week in laundry, they would do the washing and folding. I claimed I could almost guarantee that, and they gave me 25% of the profit-and they'd even do the pickup and delivery. I agreed, but said I needed enough money up front to paint the building, buy bins, and build a counter-which they did. I handed out hundreds of flyers proclaiming, "Free beer if you bring down your laundry!" We washed $300 in the first weekend alone. And on a gorgeous Saturday afternoon, many of my customers exited the shop very inebriated. I even bought an ad in The Kenyon Collegian that said, "Yep, the only student prize on Main Street!" On the receipt papers, it wrote, "If your clothes aren't coming to you, you should come to me." I had defeated all of the student laundry competitors by the time I graduated, and I was even able to sell the firm when I left Gambier. That was my true college success story.

CHAPTER V

On June 13, 1949, at 2 p.m., I graduated from Kenyon, and at 4 p.m., I landed at Williams Bay, Wisconsin. For the forthcoming season, the Belfry Players historical theatre has offered me a scholarship.

Due to my father's lack of knowledge about the usual wage for summer-stock theatrical work, he was adamant that I be paid for my efforts or turn down Belfry's offer. What he didn't realise was how many other young theatre professionals were eager to take your place if your demands were too high—or if you made any demands at all. I was as much of a professional actress as any of the other kids in the company, and they weren't. Belfry did hire (for a fee) several recent drama school graduates to establish a type of resident company, and they also managed to hire some professionals who were not at the top of their game to direct our productions. However, theatres like the Belfry didn't have much to offer other than the opportunity to perform a large number of plays in a short period of time.

The Belfry Players rented a beautiful old wooden cottage near Lake Geneva. That was where all the apprentices lived, including myself and Jackie Witte, a lovely local Wisconsin drama student I met. We frequently go to neighbourhood bars in the evening, and when the bars close, we typically sit under the door and talk about our future. Jackie aspires to be an actor. I told her about the play we were both in, John Loves Mary, and my ambitions - perhaps in an impractical and lyrical way - and she responded sweetly.

To have a friend in the theatre who you saw not only working during the day but also at night, someone who didn't have to dash back to her family, someone who would share the privilege of going out for a beer with you after a long day of building sets and rehearsing together, well, that was almost indescribable ecstasy. I'd never been with a woman I could talk to, and I'd never had the chance. Of course, there was my mother, and then, when I was seventeen, there was the war. Following the Pacific, Dorothy attended an all-male college while working at her Gambier restaurant. There were faculty spouses and their girls who performed in the plays alongside us. No one else followed until Jackie. I'd never seen someone like her before.

***

Jackie's parents lived in Beloit, but they also had a beachfront summer home near Lake Geneva that served as both a sanctuary and a hiding place. Jackie introduced me to them early on, but I wasn't sure what to think of them. Her mother was a frightened woman who darted around like a rat and never looked you in the eyes. She was wonderfully kind, but elusive, always scurrying around, busy organising bridge parties. The father was a good, decent man, thin and not too talkative, but with a dry sense of humour on occasion. I assumed he was depressed. I used to go fishing with him in his rowboat on occasion. These were beautiful days.

I suppose marrying Jackie, whom I met only a few months before, was akin to the Kenyon College Revue. I'm not sure what I was thinking while I was composing the revue, but once you committed to doing something, you just did it. I made my first meaningful contact with anyone with Jackie, and I assumed that after making that first contact with a woman, the next thing you did was get married and have a lot of kids. I wish someone, whether a priest, a social worker, or a psychiatrist, had just sat the two of us down for a minute and said, "Think this out, just follow it through, and create a script for yourselves." "Well, I'm not really sure," I would have probably said to Jackie. "How are you feeling?" "I'm not sure, either," Jackie would have responded. It was the first time either of us had had a connection with the luxury of leisure, the first time we'd ever had in a free environment. But all we did was obey a set of half-learned principles that we thought were rules. We were playing this by a book, and we were singing all the songs to music. It was as if everything had been chosen and decreed, and there was no choice but to follow the rules. You're meant to finish college, acquire a job, get married, have kids, and protect and provide for them. Beyond that, I didn't understand much. Neither Jackie nor I had an idea, not even an inkling. We never considered utilising contraception and never inquired. We had no parenting philosophy, and we'd never discussed whether or not to have children. Things happened just because they happened.

Looking back now, from a more mature perspective, I wonder how I could have been so irresponsible as to marry and conceive the first female with whom I had a verbal connection so quickly. It felt right at the time. It had a fatalistic feel to it, as if it was all predestined, preordained. You finished what you started. I had no idea I could mould things myself.

***

After we were engaged that summer, I spent some evenings at Jackie's parents' house. Jackie's room was below, while her parents' room was upstairs. I was terrified her parents might show up and surprise us. We waited till the night of our wedding. I don't recall anything about our wedding, which took place at an Episcopal church near Jackie's parents' house, save for leaving the reception afterwards. We borrowed her father's old Nash and ended up driving in a snowstorm for five or six hours. We were completely fatigued by the time we arrived at our motel. "Why don't we just rest up now?" we would have asked if we had any sense. But I believe Scott, our son, was conceived that night. The next morning, we simply awoke, got into the car, and drove in a large circle. We eventually directed the car toward Woodstock, Illinois, where we were both supposed to begin employment with a winter theatre company. We got there quite fast.

***

Despite the fact that Jackie and I were both promised positions at Woodstock, when we arrived, the sleazy gentleman who ran the theatre told us there was no room for Jackie in the group. He promised her a couple of parts, but instead employed her for ten dollars a week at the box office. As an actor, I got forty-five and was cast in a stage production of Ethan Frome and as Christian in Cyrano de Bergerac; our company's Cyrano had a southern dialect, and we almost lost our Roxane one night when her balcony started to crumble.

We rehearsed those plays in only six days, and it was hilarious. Despite the fact that the company had finished one good season and that the local community was supportive of the performances, which were held in a beautiful historic opera house, the theatre began to fall bankrupt and was unable to pay its bills. Our sleight-of-hand manager stole the money, and the Woodstock Players went bankrupt. Nonetheless, Jackie and I had this four-room furnished flat on the upper floor of this big townhouse that we rented for a few dollars a month. We received what we paid for—no running water for that amount.

I informed my father that it would most likely take another month for me to find another regular job and that I was applying for unemployment benefits. He responded to me with an utterly caustic letter. Lethal. Welfare, he said, was for individuals who couldn't work; admitting that one of his kids had gone out and collected unemployment would be a stain on the Newman family reputation.

So I got a job at a nearby farm owned by Tilley. I had to clean the barn's sheep corral. You'd cover it with clean hay after the sheep peed and spit. Then they'd pee and spit again, and you'd cover it up again. You'd ultimately clean it out when it came to be about six feet deep and virtually up to the eaves. That was my responsibility. With my allergies, I couldn't breathe by two or three o'clock in the afternoon every day. But I stayed for maybe six or seven weeks.

My father's condition was what brought me back home. He had exploratory surgery in January 1950, but I don't believe anything was done to him. His condition had progressed too far, according to the surgeons. He'd spend the remainder of his life in and out of the hospital.

I went to see him a few times while he was recovering from surgery. He still went to his sporting goods business on occasion. But, with no employment and my father's health fast deteriorating, Jackie and I travelled to Cleveland.

Jackie, Arthur, and I relocated to my parents' home. Jackie was pregnant at the time my father was dying. It was the most difficult period of my life. My mother despised Jackie, who tried to be as lovely and sweet as she could but received a beating. I believe there were two major factors that turned my mother against her. First, because she was my wife; my mother suffered from a severe illness of envy that kept her isolated. Second, Jackie's father was a butcher, and my mother intended for me to marry someone better. Jackie was viewed as a second-class citizen by her.

Jackie was a true stoic. She wasn't a complainer or a crybaby. If my mother was a monster to her, that was the way it was. Jackie had come from a home where there was little joy, so our household was not much of a change for her. What are the horrors of being alone with Tress Newman all day? A whole nightmare. Jackie felt crushed under the weight of my mother's lovely, finely controlled voice. Jackie's sole chance for protection was to understand exactly what my mother did and to do exactly what she was told. My mother was treating Jackie the same way she had always treated me. I don't even recall discussing it with Jackie. I was in Newman-Stern, working twelve-hour days at the family business. All I had to go on was rumour.

Our house was large, and it had the potential to be a lovely sanctuary. It's bad Jackie's time had to be so miserable. I don't think I recognized how horrible it was at the time.

Every evening after dinner, we'd leave the house as soon as we could and return as late as we could.

***

Even as he deteriorated, my father appeared preoccupied with his appearance-perhaps unsurprising given that he was one of the last gentlemen to wear spats on a regular basis. He lacked the power to shave himself, and he despised not being shaved. Arthur shaved him virtually every day, but one afternoon, despite Arthur's presence, my father asked me to do it. I remember wanting to be of use to him while also restraining myself. He was so delicate that I was terrified I'd cut him; we'd hardly ever touched. Soon after, when Arthur and I sat near his hospital bed, I overheard my father say, "Paul is the better shaver of you two." I can still see Arthur's sadness on his face.

My father made it obvious to Arthur and me before he died that there would be nothing in his bequest for us. We had no expectations, thus there were no disappointments. "I figure I owed it to both of you to clothe you, feed you, comfort you, and give you a decent education," that's what he's always said. "But when you reach your maturity, you're on your own."

When my father understood he was dying, he wanted to place all of his money into a trust for my mother to protect her-he did it this way because he was terrified she'd lose everything if he didn't. He suspected she was unstable. What he didn't realise was how suspicious she was, suspicious enough to suspect he was planning to deprive her of her fortune.

Tress was certain that my father had a girlfriend hidden somewhere, and that he was plotting to take her home and control of Newman-Stern away from her and give it to the "mistress." He only required her approval to his estate plan while he lay in the hospital, but she refused to sign anything. Tress continued to rage at him on his deathbed, accusing and vilifying him. She was not going to let him die!

My mother hadn't communicated with her own family in three years when my father died in May 1950. She invited everyone to the funeral. What was the point of doing that if not to show the Newman side that she, too, had friends? Was she announcing her separateness by inviting her people to our house and promptly hurrying them up the stairs, even though both families were at our house together to pay their respects-and never even returning back downstairs to offer the Newmans a cup of tea? Was it a reprimand? Was it like the child who died in her hug or her dog that was poisoned by chocolate? Emotions aroused with no regard for the consequences?

***

My father was a battleground both during his marriage and while he was dying. Did her disagreement with my father's brother, my uncle Joe, over her share of Newman-Stern, her mistrust of my father's intentions for his estate, and now the sudden inclusion of her own relatives (and exclusion of his) in the mourning period define the sheet of steel that existed between the two families? I'm wondering if this wasn't also true in their marriage. I tried to figure out what they meant to each other. My mother had always told me, "Your father and I fought a lot, but we were great in bed." Perhaps that was it, the glue, that passion. Perhaps it was because she was the pupil and my father was the willing teacher? I believe she was unaware of the devastation she had caused. My mother mourned my father after he died. I had no idea why. She'd been kicking the bejesus out of him a week before his death, accusing him of having another woman. Things had gotten rather bad in our house. Arthur refused to speak to her. Things were tense between her and Uncle Joe regarding her ownership of the store; it was difficult to persuade her that Joe was a good man. Tress, on the other hand, was taken aback when the will was ultimately read. My father had left her all he owned in Newman-Stern, including the house. "Mother, Dad always told us it's all going to you, and nothing is coming to us," Arthur and I kept assuring her. My brother and I were never forgiven by her for being correct about the will.

My father was a genuinely moral, deeply miserable man who found satisfaction in observing his own principles; he never found that joy at home. I imagine him as a funny little clown of a man who's off performing a jig somewhere, behaving exactly like me.

One of my most regrets about my father's untimely passing (he was just fifty-six) is that we never fully connected. His reaction to the realisation that eventually came to me would have been one of wonder and delight. We could have shared a lot of things, including a sense of success. He would have been proud of our friendship in a way that wasn't simply a reflection of me, his puppet, a possession, on him. He would have acknowledged and honored me. My mother saw me as a weapon of her Catholicism to be exhibited in front of my father's people as royal vindication of her own family, her intelligence, her bloodlines. My elation in my accomplishment has always been tempered by a deep melancholy that my mother could never completely share in my joy.

Most persons who have completely lived themselves remember someone-a teacher, a religious figure, a parent, uncle, grandfather-about whom they can say, "That was my mentor." That was my pillar. That's who guided me in the right direction, who encouraged me, and who set a good example for me to follow." That was never an option for me.

I've always questioned why I couldn't find a mentor. I never had someone in my upbringing that I could look back on and say, "Boy, I never realised what a foundation that was, how much I relied on that.""I got a little morality from my father; I'm not sure what I got from my mother." I'm not sure if any teachers provided me with anything or helped me comprehend myself. There was no scout leader or camp counsellor. Nobody goes to church. Nothing. As far as I know, I received no emotional assistance from anyone.

Mr. Arthur Newman

If Paul had followed my advice and gone into business, he would have been a success since he was likeable, had a fantastic personality, and made people like him right away. Furthermore, he was astute and perceptive, and he possessed all of the necessary ingredients no matter what he accomplished.

I was dissatisfied with the Newman-Stern Co. I was making approximately $75 per week, but I couldn't find any meaning in my life there. I'm not sure whether it would have been offered to me, but I had no desire to operate the store one day. The Newman-Stern Co. was sold the following May, and I went to work at a golf range managed by Newman-Stern's new owners. I stayed until the end of July, but I took money from the cash register at the driving range. It came to about $175 over three or four months; I kept track of it (and eventually reimbursed the golf range when I got a part-time job in graduate school). I'm not sure why I did that-was it for beer money or something?

I suppose I needed the extra money as well. Jackie and I had moved into a new home in Bedford, a Cleveland suburb near Shaker Heights, by the time Scott was born in September 1950. I believe I was able to purchase it-for $11,700!-because my father signed a note guaranteeing a loan soon before he died.

My new house was one storey and on a tiny corner lot, with a tiny living room, kitchen, garage, and two tiny bedrooms. Everything was brand new. There was no furniture or appliances. There were no hedges, plants, or landscaping in the front yard. I had to include them all. I went to work, came home, and we had dinner with one of the neighbours, or we went downtown to Horrigan's, a long, narrow old Irish bar where I liked to loosen up (and the very amiable proprietor would delight us by sitting down at a piano and singing "H-O-double R-I-G-A-N spells Horrigan!"). Not every day in Bedford was a joy, and not every day was a disaster.

Jackie and I were more concerned with the fact that we were having our first kid. I don't think we made as many plans as usual. We were having a baby, and it would grow like tulips on the new lawn or whatever else we planted on the earth. We were two extremely young people attempting to act mature.

I've told people that if I had one plan in life, it would be to apply to Yale School of Drama and obtain a master's degree in directing so that if I couldn't get work as an actor, I could always teach. (And I never imagined I'd be in a movie.) But, if I had planned on attending Yale in 1951, why did I buy this new house in the fall of 1950, with all that interest to pay? I wasn't planning ahead of time, so I figured I could move my family whenever I wanted, make plans, cancel plans, and nothing would be a huge issue. Adventurous? Whimsical? Uncaring?

Going to Yale was not a calculated decision. My GI Bill school benefits were about to expire; I suspected I'd had a few beers, gone off somewhere inside my skull, beat my fist, danced up and down, and yelled, "Let's go to Yale!"

I believe I imagined Yale as a flight from something that didn't provide a sense of growth or advancement. I know I wasn't sprinting madly toward the validation of theatre because I didn't expect to achieve anything professionally. Still, with a couple of minor radio and television gigs, I was making a name for myself in Cleveland. I performed a few commercials for a local bank, which was ironic because I was recommending people to save money for their children when I had never saved a dime in my life. I also did late-night TV weather. I was terrified about having to deliver lines directly into the camera. Television was brand new at the time (though my mother had one of the first sets), and I'd never done anything like that before; I still can't talk to anything that doesn't respond-it's terrifying. I'm not sure why they hired me.

I don't recall ever having a serious conversation with Jackie about going to New Haven. I submitted an application. I've been accepted. I recall it as a foregone conclusion. Let's get in the car and go.

For me, the time between my father's death and our drive to Connecticut in the Chevy was a jumble of impressions, with no clear, powerful, enduring memory. Except for becoming a father with the advent of Scott. I recall having a strong physical connection with Scott. Holding him and bouncing him, working his legs, pushing him in his perambulator up and down the street.

But the bond was more brotherly than parental, because I didn't consider myself to be a father. I now have a strong sense of omission about this, of things left unfinished or never begun. A sensation of failure. What should have been a solid father-son bond was deteriorating, a marriage was falling apart, and I had no idea. I didn't know enough about my own feelings to begin evaluating them or taking any serious actions; I felt disgusted with myself for being so ineffectual. For all of the hard work and thrill of immersion that came with my time at Yale, it was a type of purgatory, a resting place. I regard that time in my life as the start of a big failure: failure to offer relief for Jackie at the house where she lived, failure as a husband, lover, actor, and father. I make no denials. I'm not trying to appease anyone. I do, however, have a tendency to focus on the bad aspects of situations.

CHAPTER VI

The job is what I remember about Yale more than anything else. I started at nine a.m., worked until dinner, and then continued with rehearsals until about eleven p.m. You'd be performing two or three plays at once, as well as one-act plays on Saturday mornings that the Yale writers' organisation had invited the student actors and directors to perform.

This was pure theatre immersion, but there was no sense of pressure. Work that is both difficult and enjoyable. Yale had so many compatible people that you had a genuine sense of camaraderie and ease.

I planned to major in directing, but this was all a ruse. The plan was to give what I was studying some gravitas. I was persuaded that the nameplate on your door that read "Director" was superior to one that said "Actor." As previously stated, I had no real plan; yet, with directing, all I had was a parachute.

Frank McMullan, a long-time Yale faculty member, oversaw our directing studies and taught acting and phonetics. He struck me as a bit pedantic; in fact, Yale's entire approach to theatre was highly academic-we were even expected to study fencing. I'd gone down to Manhattan at one point during the semester to attempt to meet some agents; I was particularly affected by the personality, rush, stress, and urgency in their offices. Young actors were being shoved in and out of doors, and new ones were being pushed in and out. When I returned to university, I modelled a scenario for McMullan's directing class based on my experience. I acquired a garbage can and had a youngster beat on it with a stick upstage, while a typist typed away in a separate rhythm downstage, with seven or eight actors rushing around in time to the rhythms. It was a big hit with my class. When it was finished, however, Frank McMullan looked at me and asked, "Why don't we do this in a more realistic way?" Let's get rid of that beat." Of course, the performers did what he instructed. It was hilarious that what I saw as the heart of the exercise was the very thing he removed. But that's how I remember Yale.

What I remember most about Connie Welch, my major acting teacher at Yale, is everything I don't recall about my subsequent studies at the Actors Studio in New York. Her classes appeared to be choreographed, technical, prepared, and scholarly. They did not inspire me in the least.

Surprisingly, the subject at Yale that helped me the most was the History of Theater, given by Alois Nagler, a German exile. It lasted from the Greeks to great French writers such as Racine. Despite my horrible job schedule-aside from lessons and rehearsals at theatre school, I was also selling encyclopaedias for additional money-I had to read a variety of plays. As a result, I had a lot greater understanding of what constituted a good and bad play. Finally, knowing the difference between a good script and a terrible one.

***

I'd located a place for my family on New Haven's Chapel Street. It had three rooms on the third floor of a building with a furrier's business on the ground floor and a condemned second floor. We gave Scott the bedroom and Jackie and I took the screened porch, which the landlord had glassed in so he could charge for another room.

Mrs. Dupuy, another resident, also lived there. She had tapped on our door and introduced herself the first time we met; while she did so, we observed she was scratching the side of her head with a.45 Colt handgun. Mrs. Dupuy informed us she was a widow who was OK since she kept this gun by her side in case her apartment was broken into. She also mentioned that she gave off so much body heat during her marriage that it drove her late husband insane since he could never get their bed chilly enough for him to sleep.

We held parties all the time at our house. We cooked in the small kitchen and barbecued in the backyards of other married students nearby. I'd create something spectacular, such as open-faced grilled-cheese sandwiches with garlic butter, bacon, and mozzarella. People thought they were fantastic, and whenever they heard I was cooking them, they flocked to my house in droves. (I tried cooking them again lately, and they actually tasted pretty horrible.) We never had much money, so we all bought meals together to save money.

In the summer, we'd have picnics every Sunday in a lovely little place along the Merritt Parkway. Scott was charming and the focus of attention. Everyone would bring their own small children, and we'd play with them beside a local creek.

I liked having so many people around. We had a great time in New Haven. Probably the greatest of our family times, the best of Jackie and my lives.

Ed Levy, a close friend of Paul's at Kenyon and of both Paul's and Jackie's in New York.

Paul asked my parents and aunt to see Picnic and agreed to meet us for a drink afterward. He brought Joanne with him. She was excited to be there, satisfied. She felt joyful since she was falling in love with Paul and just waited for things to happen. Joanne claimed she was terrified to walk home alone because it was unsafe; Paul said he would see her home, and they departed. My aunt told me, "She's kinda sweet to him."

"No, there's nothing to it," I responded.

I refused to believe it was anything; I'd never suspected Paul of having an affair since he was kind of straight-the way guys who had recently married were back then.

When I saw Paul and Jackie together later that evening, I whispered to him, "Oh, tell me about Joanne Woodward." "I believe she may be living with someone." And what I meant was, would she be willing to date me? "I have that feeling, too," Jackie added, "about her living with someone." But she said it with a smirk.

Paul slumped down in his chair because he definitely hadn't told me. I believe he'd been dropping hints, but I refused to accept them because I didn't want to give up my vision of Paul. We'd go out drinking and he'd remark, "You know, I met this girl in a bar..." I couldn't believe it was anything more than him talking.

I ran across Paul and Joanne a few years later in Detroit, where Joanne was performing in a play called The Lovers. Paul was still married at the time, and I believe he'd just had his third child with Jackie. I was always loyal to Paul. I told him I didn't think he was a jerk, that I saw what he saw in Joanne, and that I could tell when something wasn't right with Jackie. Paul responded with a note. "You're the only one," remarked the man, "who doesn't think I'm a shit."

Jackie and I chose to relocate from Staten Island to a rental in Fresh Meadows, near the Queens/Nassau County boundary, about the time Picnic debuted. By then, I was often going out after our shows to one of our show bars with cast members like Meeker, Janice Rule, and Kim Stanley. But in my view, it was mostly Joanne and myself. There would also be some college buddies of mine or hers, TV personalities-every night, a lot of people around us. Joanne had a fourth-floor walkup studio on the East Side; it was only one room with a built-in kitchenette, so we'd frequently end up nearby, such as at Costi's. Was Jackie sceptical of what was going on? I'm not sure; Jackie was the only person who was more naive than I was.

As the run of Picnic came to a conclusion, I wasn't sure what to do next; there had been talk about starring in some TV shows and other Broadway shows, and Hollywood had also approached me. Josh Logan advised me not to sign up for cinema tickets. "Well, listen," my agent, Maynard Morris, replied. It's fine if you don't want to go to LA. But keep in mind that people will wait and wait and knock on your door again and again until one day there will be no more knocking. "You never know when that last knock will come." And the last knock I heard was for The Silver Chalice. Years later, when my career had progressed considerably, I was frequently reported as declaring it was "the worst movie produced in the fifties": this was not an incorrect statement.

***

My time in California did not start off well. I drove there alone from New York, with no idea where I was heading. I was supposed to stay at the Roosevelt Hotel in Hollywood, but I got off at the incorrect exit on one of the freeways-I'm not sure if it was the Ventura or the Pasadena; I must have cut all the way across Kansas. Anyway, I don't recall ever arriving in Los Angeles, but I did wind up exiting at Santa Monica Boulevard. Of course, I eventually discovered that there was a far easier way to go where I was going, but I had to drive a great distance on local Sunset roads. It seemed like an eternity until I discovered Roosevelt.

The Silver Chalice was being shot on the Warner Bros. property in Burbank, but I had a meeting at MGM at the other end of town early on. I nearly ran over a lady pushing a baby carriage who was crossing the street. I began yelling, "You dumb shit!" "You almost ran over that woman in a crosswalk!" yelled a cop as he pulled me over.

"What was wrong about that?"

"In Los Angeles, pedestrians have the right of way." "So, where are you from?"

Before I could respond, he recognized my New York licence plates and asked for my licence. "It's being sent out from New York; I just got here but I left my wallet at home." I wasn't locked up for some reason.

***

The Silver Chalice was a big-budget biblical toga epic about a young silversmith (me) who was tasked with creating the Holy Grail after Jesus died. The director was Victor Saville, whose films dated back to the silent era and who had spent years putting this film together. During the few rehearsals we really had, I understood I wasn't going to get any assistance from Victor, whom I must have driven insane.

Arthur Park became Paul's primary movie agent at MCA.

He was nothing like himself when he performed The Silver Chalice. Because he despised it. He despised the part, despised the way it was being played, and the fact that he'd fallen into what he saw as a trap. It was excruciatingly uncomfortable for him, and he was cursing himself for allowing himself to get into this predicament.

John Foreman, Paul's agent and later business partner

Every studio sought Paul after he opened Picnic. He was the hottie. And the reason "coast" (what we dubbed our LA office) chose Warner Bros. was because Paul had the opportunity to star in his debut film, plus they gave the greatest terms. Everyone went into The Silver Chalice with their eyes wide open, even Paul Newman, who was thanking the gods above for the chance to make some real money at the time of the deal. He'd move from $350 to $400 a week on Broadway to $1,750 per week to begin at Warners.

Meade Roberts, a screenwriter best known for his collaborations with Tennessee Williams on the fugitive kind and summer and smoke, was close to both Joanne and Paul in the 1950s.

Paul told me before leaving for Hollywood that he was really worried about the Silver Chalice role. "No Bible movie is ever a flop," Maynard Morris said to Paul. "Take a look at what The Robe did for Richard Burton!"

Paul responded, "I don't think The Silver Chalice is The Robe."

Meade Roberts

A few months after the release of Chalice, I met up with Paul at a tavern we loved on Fifty-fourth and Sixth, directly across from the old Ziegfeld. Jimmy Dean was seated right inside.

Dean's future film was already widely publicised.

"Oh, Paul, you poor guy!" Jimmy exclaimed. Look at yourself! "Have you heard about how wonderful East of Eden is?" He became sarcastic and just plain awful.

Paul accepted it with grace and dignity. I'd have smacked him. I was dying too.

CHAPTER VII

Making The Silver Chalice became a metaphor for me for the entire movie industry, its failure, hollowness, and superficiality. I suppose it was only fitting that it would be my first film and that it would fail miserably. And it would be appropriate that I would be negotiating to return to New York and do another Broadway play before the film was even finished filming, sensing the calamity of it, sensing the amateurishness of it. Thus began my fight to free myself from this vision from which I couldn't get away. But, to paraphrase Theodore Roosevelt, I would tread it underfoot on the one hand, but not so quickly on the other.

I'm not referring to my success (or lack thereof), but rather to my physical appearance. It is not straightforward. My appearance was what got me in the door. What would I have done if I looked like Golda Meir? Nowhere; it was like being a guy with a trust fund who doesn't have to work. I've always had a trust fund for my appearance. That would suffice. But I understood I needed something more to survive. Especially when my life appeared to be shifting once more.

Mary Hara, nicknamed Blatz, a friend of Paul's from Yale's directing program

Paul had just returned to town from filming The Silver Chalice, and he took me to watch Gate of Hell, a Japanese samurai film.

"What was it like in Hollywood?" I inquired. "Did you enjoy doing it?"

"Blatz," Paul replied, "out there, they'll do anything for money." They'll do anything for money, even kill for it. It's really terrible."

Joanne (who'd also been working at the time) and I had a terrible quarrel when I left Hollywood after Silver Chalice wrapped.

Everything was over between us. We resolved never to see each other again. I opted to go back to New York because my mother was visiting and I planned to drop her off in Cleveland. (We even stopped in Vegas for a terrific all-you-can-eat meal for a dollar.)

Joanne was in a bad predicament since she was a backstreet wife and I refused to divorce her. I didn't know how I'd do it, but I wanted to attempt to mend my marriage and spend time with my family. That thought pervaded my mind, and after I left California, Joanne and I didn't speak or connect for what seemed like months.

I began rehearsals for the Broadway production of The Desperate Hours, in which I portrayed an escaped criminal who kidnaps Karl Malden and his family. After it became a big play, Jackie and I decided to rent a property in Sea Girt, New Jersey, which is only an hour and fifteen minutes from Manhattan. There were a lot of Grosse Pointe/Shaker Heights-style mansions about a block from the beach, and in the middle of them all was a Charles Addams house that was unfinished on the inside and falling apart on the outside. It was incredible.

Sea Girt's surf was large and wonderful. Every night after the play, I'd travel there and swim in the breakers at midnight. I felt at ease in those encompassing waves that knocked you down, the lovely sensation of being surrounded in that raging sea.

Strangely, despite nearly drowning as a child, I was never afraid of water. I'm not sure how old I was, but I was in the local pool and couldn't swim. There was a counsellor and maybe a hundred and fifty youngsters in the huge pool with him. Six of us would all hop on his back at the same time, and he'd wade out into the water up to his shoulders—and over my head. I just dropped off and sank one afternoon. Completely gone. I grabbed hold of another counsellor's waist and wouldn't let go when he came swimming by-I remember the flash of his bathing suit. I was submerged around his belt, but the counsellor assumed I was just messing about, so he dunked me anytime I managed to surface. He eventually grabbed it, bringing me to the side of the pool as I was about to drown. I couldn't have gone on much longer. With all that chaos, I would have simply slid to the bottom, and someone would have subsequently quipped, "Well, isn't that funny? Some kid's down there looking for pennies at the pool's bottom!"

Jackie and I had a fantastic weekend at Sea Girt. Scott was probably four or five years old at the time, and our first daughter, Susan, was still a toddler; it was a fantastic time for them as well. We'd always bring folks to my weekend-which was Sunday to Monday since there were no Sunday matinees back then-and I'd cookouts and everyone would go down to the beach for swimming.

Then, back in town, I went to a script reading at some producer's home, and there she was, coming out of an adjacent office. We just stood there staring at one other, and it was back on.

Then it was back on track.

There were additional separations and breakups, and we were not always together. Terrible battles. But, after a while, I had to return to Warners in California for meetings. Joanne was already in Hollywood, working on a television project for 20th Century Fox. Within the Warner Bros. lot, there is a lengthy boulevard that runs by dressing rooms, parking lots, an administration building, an executive dining room, and the commissary, which Joanne was just leaving one day. We somehow noticed one other and yelled from four blocks away; then, as in a movie, we began rushing toward each other, arms spread. It was incredible.

I reached a point when I was living two lives. I was living my life with Jackie, and Joanne was enjoying hers. These were difficult times. I'd never had a feeling of repercussions before, nor had I ever suffered from them. I enlisted for a torpedo bomber and made it out alive. I graduated from college without having worked. After drinking too much beer, I drove my car off a cliff. But with Jackie and Joanne, the implications started to weigh hard on me. As an adulterer, I was a failure.

My personal problems were not interfering with my professional life. I was cast in The Battler, an hour-long live TV drama directed by Arthur Penn and based on one of Hemingway's Nick Adams novels about a punch-drunk ex-boxing champion who tragically chooses the glory of the ring above the love of a loyal woman. Jimmy Dean was cast as the lead, and I was cast as the principal supporting actor. Jimmy was killed two weeks before the episode was to air when his Porsche crashed on a minor highway in California. The decision was reached to proceed, and I assumed Jimmy's role as the fighter.

It was draining. There were three rehearsals every day, from eight a.m. to ten p.m. A practice run. A dress rehearsal with clothing changes and makeup—my character had to go from beat-up to handsome to beat-up again during a live sixty-minute show; I was having prosthetics glued on and removed from my face at breakneck speed. I went out with an executive from our show's sponsor, Pontiac, and our producer, Fred Coe, after we finished preparing the night before. I had two glasses of beer and became extremely shaky. And as we exited this Sunset Strip eatery and waited for the valet to fetch our car, Coe and the adman observed a nice automobile idling nearby and decided to have some fun by filling one of its hubcaps with gravel. Some youngster, the owner, came out of the restaurant, got into that car, and drove away-and the transmission immediately fell out.

He leaped out of the car and charged at us, yelling, "Who did that?" Fred Coe directed his finger at me. The boy rushes over, punches me in the face, gets back in his car, and drives away. I returned to my room at the Chateau Marmont, where Joanne had been staying, and I was laughing. "I'm a middleweight champion, and I'm standing there with both hands in my pockets when a kid crawls up on an orange crate and belts me in the eye." "I had no idea what hit me." Everyone wanted to know how I got the nasty whack on my face during the next few days. I made up a story about my co-star Frederick O'Neal hitting me too hard with his shoe during an action scene; thank God, I added, it didn't bloom until after we'd finished filming the show. I can't tell you how impressed they were that I'd been injured while on duty.

The Battler received a lot of great feedback, especially from director Bob Wise, who was preparing to make the major Rocky Graziano biopic, Somebody Up There Likes Me. Graziano was a true American sports hero, a rugged New Yorker who clawed his way up from the slums and juvenile prisons to become a champion, a world championship holder. The picture was supposed to be Jimmy Dean's next production, and his sudden death certainly messed things up; Wise and the producers hired me, most likely based on my performance in The Battler.

I'm aware that some people attribute my professional successes to Jimmy's death. Yes, there were elements of luck, and much of my success has been due to what I term "Newman's luck." When I was born white in America in 1925, Newman's luck began. The second luck is one's appearance. The third luck is cognitive ability in innovating. And I had the good fortune to overcome the fact that people always said to me, "Isn't he darling!" or "Isn't he so cute!" by having the determination to understand that I wasn't going to be able to subsist on that alone. I'd encountered indifference, stupidity, and my own lack of perception. But I'd never actually experienced serious difficulty. Luck recognized my face.

Half of me says, "You could have done it anyway if Jimmy hadn't been killed." It would have taken a little longer, but it would have happened."

Robert Wise was the director of somebody up there like me.

James Dean had agreed to appear in the picture. But, before the script could be completed, he died in an awful accident. The only other actor we considered was John Cassavetes; I had lunch with him at the MGM commissary and told him I thought he was too small for the character, especially stripped down. He was irritated and stated that any real actor can act anything, including his size.

Paul was on the set, having just finished The Rack, and the studio suggested I view some sequences. He was great, therefore it was decided he'd be the one.

Paul and I agreed that since Rocky was still alive, and Paul shared my belief that you should dig and research as much as you can about a character, we should spend time in New York with Rocky. We didn't want it to be a carbon replica of Rocky with flaws around the edges, but whatever Rocky Paul could acquire for himself.

Rocky brought us to all of his favourite spots on the Lower East Side, including the pigeon keepers on the roofs and his neighbourhood candy store. Rocky would sometimes go ahead of us, and Paul would watch his gait and observe he had rounded heels on his shoes, which gave him a peculiar shift. He carried his hands in his pockets. Paul brought his language, vocabulary, cadence, and speech pattern to the coast with him for the shoot.

I believe Paul felt safe in the fact that he had met the man he would represent and would be able to draw on him, both physically and mentally. It instilled faith in Paul.

CHAPTER VIII

Popularity can be classified into two categories. There's the intrusive side that offends your private life-what happens in the New York Post and garbage publications. It's the people who stand in front of a theatre drawing attention to the fact that you're there when you don't want any attention drawn to you. People who follow you inside libraries and your apartment building's lobby, people with flashbulbs, and nasty people.

Some consumers believe that purchasing a movie ticket entitles them to voting stock in your firm. And they don't understand why they can't simply walk up to your back door and say, "Get me a job!" or "You're so big and I'm so small, why don't you make me big, too?" These are the people who can only talk about blue eyes and externals. Those are the aspects of popularity that irritate me and cause frequent interference.

But another crucial feature of popularity is how it develops a kind of power that can be transferred to business and thus provides leverage to execute the kinds of initiatives you want to do. And as your popularity quotient falls, so does your capacity to exert the kind of pressure required to produce the films you want to be a part of.

I'd prefer to lose one half of my popularity, but if you lose one half, you lose the other as well.

Lucille Newman

Tress was cared for by my own very personal doctor at the end, and he was discreetly assisting us in getting Paul into the hospital. "This country is ridiculous," I said. This man is doing something he enjoys. Why does he have to be bothered so much? Why can't he just live his life? It alone exists in this country." "Lucille, I was in Spain and I saw a five- or six-story building with a picture of him on the side," the doctor explained. It is not limited to this country."

Smiling for the cameras is a smile that comes from nowhere other than a command; it has no mirth. When Joanne and I were in Cannes, for example, walking up this flight of stairs with a fifteen-foot-wide red carpet and hearing music from Star Wars or whatever it is at decibels that fry your eardrums...well, you get a sense of how the kings of England must have felt at their coronations. And then you say to yourself, "They should do this for me once a day, rush me in, get the trumpets, cue the cameras, applause, and band," simply to restore your confidence. Every day as you come down from your shower, you could start your day with the fucking fanfares and flashbulbs going off between the bathroom and the breakfast area. The duality is that it is both a dream and a nightmare.

When Joanne and I travelled to Paris to film a few scenes for Mr. and Mrs. Bridge, there were photographers at the airport, and Joanne told me, "Don't be a jerk. Pose for them, and they'll abandon us." So you agree to stand there for a minute or two, smile, hold your wife's arm, and say, "I'll see you, goodbye." Then you walk to your car, and roughly two-thirds of them follow you and do precisely what you were trying to avoid. They have no respect for anyone, and they even chase the car.

When we arrive at the Ritz, we see the same group of photographers. What was the point of my airport photo op? I'm now enraged, and I go into the hotel manager's office, demanding, "You've got to give us some way to get in and out of here." I require a back door for use in the morning." Especially since, after I leave the Ritz, I can put on a baseball cap and no one will recognize me; Joanne and I can travel wherever we choose. I'm now yelling at the Ritz personnel, "You make those fucking guys leave us alone!"

They eventually showed us an old service elevator with a sort of

French-doors-style window that leads to a backstreet behind the hotel. We were up for it. So Joanne and I wake up the next morning, ready to flee, and there isn't a single photographer in sight at the gate. So I felt like a schmuck after my horrific outburst.

One of the reasons I always felt Brando was interesting was because he pioneered an attitude in the world of performers that did not know the Hollywood studio hierarchy. The employers, the gossip columnists, the publicists: he was the first to deviate from what everyone thought was a must-interviews, ass kissing, and "movie etiquette." Marlon declared that these standards did not apply to him and that they were stupid, sentimental regulations. And he ended up leading a parade of other actors who shared his sentiments.

Michael Brockman was a close friend of Paul's. he was a highly regarded race car driver who also later became an actor and stuntman.

We were enjoying dinner-Paul, Bob Sharp, and his race crew, perhaps sixteen of us-when this lady leans over, pulls Paul, turns his head towards hers, and attempts to kiss him on the lips. He stood up, ready to strike her, then stopped and sat down. "Jesus. "What would you do?" he wondered. It was like deflating a balloon. It completely destroyed his night.

You work hard at your craft and grow slowly and painfully, and you're just getting to the point where you're starting to feel good about yourself—and not just the way you look—when someone says, "Oh, God, take off your sunglasses so I can see your baby blue eyes!" All of the self-esteem you've worked so hard to achieve is shattered. If I approached someone and said, "Let me see your brassiere," they would be extremely offended.

The dark glasses aren't merely for concealment; the situation is significantly more complicated. I have poor tolerance for light, and wearing them has made my eyes worse. There's also a buildup of Budweiser and damage from my early days of filmmaking; back then, the slower film exposures often forced an actor to stay looking straight into an arc light. To keep our eyes bright and white for the cameras, we had to put ice on them and implant stinging drops. It's not something you want to do all the time, especially if you have light-coloured eyes.

Some people are irritated that I won't sign autographs or pose for photos-or even provide a stock answer other than no. But do you have to invent a reaction to their silliness and then repeat it every time it occurs? Doesn't a person's patience wear thin after four or five repetitions of this?

It would make my life so much easier if every time someone stopped me on the street and said, "Ooh, let me take your picture," I said okay. But that would bring another twelve people over, and then some more, and you'd be standing there signing autographs and politely asking them about their mother and father. It would be fantastic if I could do that and not care; I'd feel a lot better at the end of the day.

I wish I could, but I am unable to. But I wish I could ski as well. And I wish I was good at tennis. I wish I could do more, but I can't—and that doesn't make me a horrible person.

James Goldstone directed winning, starring Paul and Joanne.

On a Sunday night, Paul, Joanne, and I went to a "secret" restaurant near Westport. They seat us in the corner, and an older woman at a nearby table notices Paul and Joanne, just as everyone else in the restaurant did. This woman suddenly brings her chair over to our table, sets it between the Newmans, and sits.

Paul looked at her and performed one of his fantastic takes, and he just stared at her for an age. "Lady, you are the fucking rudest person I've fucking ever met in this world," he says. I'm sitting here with my wife and a buddy, and you slide your chair over and place it directly between us? "What gives you the fucking goose?"

The woman swiftly backed away.

Stewart stern

One of the things I've often mentioned to Paul while we've been going down the street is how awful it is that he won't glance back at people who are staring at him. I'm glowing by the time we've gone two blocks, and I find myself smiling just because people are happy to see him. And it's something Paul won't notice because he refuses to look.

When I first met Paul in 1954, he had no concept of his public persona. People continued to mistake him for Marlon Brando and approach him for Brando's autograph (which he occasionally signed!). He was more reserved at times, more garrulous at others, and less succinct.

Paul has become increasingly mysterious over time. In communication, he has evolved from a Rubens to a Giacometti, a distillation to the fewest words imaginable. He speaks in fortune cookies, and the beginning and end are sometimes the same because there is a lull in between where an even more private procedure occurs. Even in words, he stays beyond the privacy moat.

Here are two examples that demonstrate what I mean. I had actively supported Jimmy Carter's 1976 campaign, and I was appointed as one of the United States' representatives to the UN's disarmament conference early in his presidency.

One afternoon, I paid a visit to the White House with several National Security Council colleagues. I was strolling down the corridor when I ran into the president.

"Why don't you come up with me to the Oval Office?" Carter inquired. I followed him upstairs, and let me tell you, what happened next was quite unpleasant. I've never felt comfortable among those in positions of power. But, while I was curious as to why he'd just opted not to address the UN on this matter, each time I brought it up, all the president wanted to know was how movies were made.

Paul at the united nations conference on nuclear disarmament, 1978

Let's fast forward to 1982. By then, I was fully immersed in motor racing, and I absolutely enjoyed the fact that it was a world away from the film industry and Hollywood.

I'd gone out to Brainerd, Minnesota, for a Trans Am race, my first professional competition. Because it was still a novelty that a movie actor was racing, there were photographers everywhere. The track marshals began pushing everyone away from the cars and racers just as we were about to start. But, just as it got down to "Gentlemen, start your engines," there was one photographer who kept snapping away at me, withdrawing for a minute, then darting back on the track like a bird.

Now, I don't want to exaggerate, but this was the period before any race when you like to get rid of all the extraneous distractions and focus on what you have to do: think through your strategy, how you want to start, what car in front of you, what's its horsepower, and where you can gain an advantage-catch them in the first turn, say, sneak in a little late? This is when a driver has to centre himself, and here comes this photographer, almost up my nose, clicking, darting off, darting back on, and finally gone.

After the marathon, when I had finished being interviewed and everyone was packing up, I approached the photographer and said, "I really want to ask you something." Why did you want to shoot me so badly that you had to come back and annoy me, violate my space, and do one more thing to make your presence known?"

"You really want to know?" said the photographer.

"Yes, I really want to know."

"Okay," he replied. "Because I thought I might get the last picture of you alive."

Patty Newman was Arthur Newman's wife, Paul's sister-in-law.

Tress was nearing the end of her life, and we'd gathered at her bedside when the special nurse we'd hired called to say it was almost time. She was deep asleep, and there were long pauses between her breaths. We immediately hurried to the side of her bed, but she was no longer there.

Joanne phoned and requested to speak with Paul. I asked her to wait a minute.

"What is he doing?"

"If you can believe it," I said to her, "he's signing a picture for the nurse."

My divorce had been finalised by the time I began pre production for The Long, Hot Summer near Baton Rouge in 1957. That allowed Joanne and me to be together freely. But, because the tale of my marital divorce wouldn't be in the media for a few months, and because the press-at least in those days-didn't magically appear everywhere you went, we were able to avoid any frenzy.

Joanne and I had met backstage at Picnic over four years ago; the fact that we would eventually get to work together again in Long, Hot Summer meant everything. I portrayed a rakish vagrant who goes to work for a rich, powerful family dictator (played by Orson Welles) in the film, which was partially inspired by a William Faulkner tale. My drifter and Welles's daughter, Joanne, have a lot of chemistry. People have said that this was the first time I showed eroticism in a film, but if that's true, I credit it entirely to working with Joanne. My sexuality had never existed before.

For the first time, Joanne and I were able to accomplish in public what we had wished to do for years, as well as display what we had previously discovered between us. There was a glue that bound us together back then and for the rest of our lives. And the glue was this: anything appeared to be conceivable. The good, the terrible, and the fantastic. Some things were doable with everyone else, but not everything. The promise of everything was there from the start for us.

We had a great experience making that movie together. The film required a lot of effort, a long schedule, and was shot on location in extremely hot conditions because it was the end of summer in Louisiana. But on Saturday nights, Joanne and I would go to New Orleans and stroll through the French Quarter, where we felt completely at ease. It was a feast for the senses. I was wide-eyed since I'd never gone anywhere else than New York, Boston, and Los Angeles. She exposed me to the world of antiques and antique stores, and we even purchased a brass bed there.

There's also a dog. We were walking through the Quarter early one Sunday morning when we heard all this yapping behind us. We turned around to see this tiny little dog being carried by a length of yarn in the hand of some person. He was around the size of my fist.

"Good lord, what exactly is that?" we inquired. "It's a chihuahua.", "Well, he's a fierce little bugger," that's what I said."I raise 'em," the man explained. "Is this little fellow for sale?"

He said yes, and I paid sixty dollars for him.

The man handed me the puppy and told me, "You'll be able to keep him in your pocket for the rest of his life."

That dog grew up to be the size of a small truck, as you might expect. El Toro was his nickname.

El Toro was a mutt in truth, but I adored him. He was a mischievous dog. One of the most appealing aspects about him was the oft-told anecdote about how he disliked my former business colleague John Foreman. El Toro would slink out of the room whenever John arrived by my place. And El Toro once took a dump on John's hat after he left it on the bed.

Orson Welles' attendance at the shoot was also remarkable. He was aloof and seemed uneasy with Actors Studio personnel, including our director, Marty Ritt (with whom I later did Hombre, Paris Blues, The Outrage, Hemingway's Adventures of a Young Man, and Hud), and Tony Franciosa.

Orson couldn't grasp screen generosity, in which one actor lets another actor in his part obtain the greatest camera shots. Orson's lexicon does not include the phrase "screen generosity." Orson asked Marty if he could have a private chat with him after a lot of retakes on a scene he did with me. They took a step back together, as if they were debating something important. When they returned, we took another take, and I asked Marty what was going on.

"Orson thought you were undermining him," he remarked, implying that someone was stealing his screen time.

Orson had been dragging his section of the scene so that I would have less screen time than he did. At the Actors Studio, we thought that the camera should foster a sense of camaraderie among the cast members. Tony performed a fantastic job when Ritt shot the big scene when Franciosa's character keeps searching for a nonexistent hidden treasure alongside Welles' barn; he was forceful, organic, and unpredictable. After that, Orson went over to Marty and remarked, "My God, I feel old, like I've been riding a tricycle in a barrel of molasses."

Marty became recognized in Hollywood after the film's success as "the man who tamed Orson Welles." Whether true or not, I know Marty assisted me throughout rehearsals. He'd make me remove any nonsense from my performance. He'd make sure you had a sentence, an intention, or an active verb to employ in your situation.

Marty was excellent with actors, being kind and gentle. He realised that whatever worked best for the actor was likely to work best for the role as well. He'd make noises, flare his nostrils, and ask, "Well, what do you think, kid?" or "Isn't that funny?" Marty, who was once an all-state football tackle and a bigger guy, was also the most elegant person on two feet. He was a joker; he was fanciful; he'd do a waltz with an imaginary girlfriend. He was like Zero Mostel in that he could tiptoe across a floor and barely make a sound.

The issue for me with a man like Marty, and especially later in my career with John Huston, was that I believed I had to act in a specific manner to please them. So anything I provided was phoney since it wasn't a genuine answer from my core. That is still the case now, because I am unsure of what my true core is. I'm not good around those in positions of power. Even thinking about it makes my hands sweat.

CHAPTER IX

In 1959, Joanne gave birth to our first child, Nell, in California. I recall crying for the first time as an adult when I saw Joanne in the hospital that day, ashen, with a parched mouth and laying on a stretcher, heading into an elevator on her way to the delivery room. I was taken aback.

I got my camera out when Lissy was born a few years later and snapped billions of pictures. Joanne returned from the hospital wearing this bellhop hat and very nice clothing; she appeared to be worth sixty or seventy million dollars. We took Nellie in to see her new baby sister, and the first picture I have of her is her leaning over the cot, a look of pure loathing on her face. Next, I took a sequence of photos in which Joanne held the baby in her arms while Nell sat next to her, making a gargoyle expression. But then something happened: Nell transformed from gargoyle to joyful mother-in-law, a grandma with a smile that stretched from one ear to the other, over the next few pictures. It was an amazing transformation. When I look at those photos, I remember how Joanne handled the entry of our babies into our household with such grace and thoughtfulness.

Scott was born a decade ago in Shaker Heights to Jackie and me at a tough time-between my father's death and my departure for Yale. It's all jumbled up in my consciousness, muted greys that appeared to leave no imprint; I have no lasting recall of Jackie's pregnancy or her actual birth. I remember driving her to the Cleveland hospital in my family's car.37 Packard for Scott's delivery, but I honestly don't remember bringing him home.

Warren Cowan, the cofounder of the PR firm Rogers & Cowan, managed publicity for Paul and Joanne for almost forty years.

For many years, Joanne refused to go on site or make a film unless it was with Paul. She did very few films following The Three Faces of Eve, after they married, and after they divorced. And for many years, I thought the marriage was working because Joanne was still there. Because her spouse was Paul Newman, and she was doing everything she could to keep the marriage together. Now I'm convinced that the reverse is true. Paul is still fighting because of Joanne. I just think he's head over heels in love with her.

Over the next few years, Joanne and I made a conscious decision to bring the kids with us when we went on location to film a movie. In reality, for many years when the kids were young, we only rented in Los Angeles, finally purchasing a home in Coldwater Canyon after around five years together. Joanne and I recently counted the houses we'd all lived in, either on the West Coast or in New York—and that doesn't even include the two houses we've had in Connecticut (when I look back on my career, the only reason I know I've made so many movies is because I've lived in so many houses). For a tiny family, that was a lot of movement.

We had no idea that residing in so many different locales may be harmful to the children. It may have given them strength in some areas, but it did not allow them to keep a consistent network of friends.

We took Nell to several schools when she was little, and she chose the Montessori in Santa Monica. So we registered her there, and about a week later I drove over to speak with the teachers and see what was going on. When I arrived, she was at recess, so I went outside to observe her. There were groups of four or six youngsters playing, and then there was Nellie. She was standing alone, pigeon-toed, hands in front of her, pulling on her fingernails as if waiting to be called to dance. There was something courageous, anticipatory, and attentive about her, as if she was observing everyone else with hope. I completely broke down and started crying.

I know Joanne and I travelled more with Nell than with the other kids. She came to Israel when I was filming Exodus, and she was with us for a shoot in Paris shortly thereafter, as well as in London. But by the time our last kid, Clea, was born in 1969, we'd determined they'd spend the entire school year in California.

Eva Marie Saint was Paul's co-star in the Otto preminger film Exodus, filmed in Israel in 1960.

I travelled to the area with my spouse, two children, mother, father, and mother-in-law. Joanne and Paul were there, as was tiny Nell, whom I adored. Nell always wore tiny white dresses, little white heels, and tiny white gloves. She was dressed entirely in white. I was continually pointing her out to my two-year-old Laurette, saying, "Look how cute little Nell looks." So similar to Joanne! Of course, once Laurette put on an Israeli blue hat and those tiny blue shorts, we couldn't take them off.

Paul was not feeling well. He was dissatisfied with how the shoot was going. Preminger would promise script modifications, then shoot the sequences exactly as they were written.

So much time and work was put into choreographing ships and crowd scenarios. Because it was a love story, much more time should have been spent on the intimate parts, yet they were all done in one or two takes. Otto was busy making the film for a fee and had promised to United Artists to finish it for a specific amount of money-and I believe any overages came out of his pocket. He was under so much pressure to finish on time that he couldn't think about anything else except having those pages shot on time.

Otto didn't appreciate the way Paul was holding me or touching me in the huge love scene I played with Paul's character. He decided to go inside and show Paul how it was done! I was devastated and humiliated. I believe Paul simply took it, but I thought to myself, "Oh my God, what are we talking about here?"

Did settling down with the kids in one place make anything better? I'm always afraid of acknowledging failure. To not be adequate, to not being correct. I am confronted with the horrifying realisation that I know nothing. I have a lot of reservations about stuff. I have gut feelings about things, even if I can't justify them academically. And there are a lot of things about myself that I don't understand. But I am certain that no one can always be held accountable for the actions of others. You can only be responsible for yourself. I'm terrified of standing in front of people. But I just do it. If other people-say, one's children-don't do it, well, that's what they are, not what they don't do. But I know that in the arena of being, of doing something, I am able to accomplish what should be a man's first order-to provide food and clothing for his family.

I should've been more consistent with my kids. I could have been more forgiving. I could have waited a little longer. I couldn't have left on location. I could have quit my job.

Some things I could have done better. I could have done much worse.

Stephanie recently told me she recalled coming to visit Joanne and me at our Long Island Sound house when she was a kid. When the kids were asleep, I'd approach their beds, lean over, and ask, "Oh, what's this?" "How about a bag of potatoes?" And I'd pick them up and carry them about like sacks on my back. I hadn't remembered doing wonderful things like that, which were unusually my and unusually physical.

Dede Allen was a much-celebrated film editor, who'd earned multiple Oscar nominations.

I recall Paul cooking. That they did their own food has always pleased me. There were many small children. Nell was the eldest of those three, shy and quiet, and I recall Lissy, when she was six, sitting in her father's lap with her arm around his head. I recall a lot of affection and tactile sensation.

Michael Brockman

I watched him with the girls today, with Lissy and Clea and Nell, and I recall how he appeared to love and get a lot out of watching them do what they did and play and be themselves when I first met them at the race track years ago when they were still tiny girls. He's a very loving and caring person.

I'd eventually feel hurt and silly for not realising my son, Scott, could not want to ride in a race car or on a horse like me. It's weird to think about it now, but as a youngster, I never wanted to ride a horse because I was terrified of them. Scott was a strong young man who seemed to embrace danger and was fascinated with horses and ponies. But I never thought to ask him, "Scott, would you like to ride a horse?" It's also not a big problem if you don't want to do it."

It's the kind of error I've made before. Joanne and I gave a Fourth of July party at our Benedict Canyon house for the casts and crews of the two films we had just finished shooting, Hud (for me) and Bill Inge's The Stripper (for her), when Stephanie was approximately seven. I decided to attempt something a little different for all the youngsters in attendance-a professionally performed ghost story. We used the little cottage behind the pool as our theatre, and I solicited the services of Brandon deWilde, who had just played my nephew, Lonnie, in Hud, and our old friend, actor Bob Webber. We'd dimmed the lights, made the space creepy, and applied some significant makeup on Brandon's and Bob's faces-along with a lot of ketchup as blood. I presented a story about a deceased skier returning to haunt certain friends and rivals. And the plan was for Bob Webber, with blackened teeth, a whitened face, and some wig from Joanne, to reach through an open window and grab Brandon and take him away at the appropriate point in the story.

At Bob's cue, the kids all squealed with glee, but Stephanie suddenly exclaimed, "I'm terribly terrified! This is not something I want to see. "I'm terrified to death!" We came to a complete stop, turned on the lights, and Brandon sat beside Steffi, repeating, "I'm okay, look at me, I'm okay." It had an effect on her. And I think I'm stupid enough that I never realise when the line between delight and horror is crossed.

Stewart Stern

When Paul was directing Rachel, one of the decisions she had to make was whether or not to include the scene in which tiny Rachel goes in and witnesses her father embalming the body of a little boy. Paul suddenly refused to shoot it. He was worried about Nell (the young Rachel) seeing it and what it might do to her. She was only about eight years old, at a time when you're not sure how much she knew about death....When he left, he had actually completed the setup in the cellar. But we encouraged him to reconsider. Then he wanted to hang a lot of bicycles and stuff between where Nell would be and where the actual embalming was going on, whether for the aesthetics of the piece or to keep her safe.

I don't have a natural talent for fathering. Then there's the fame factor; being a movie star means you've already got three strikes against you. The adoration, the acknowledgment at restaurants-these are utterly alien conditions. It's not like owning a baseball club, where you can take your kids to the beach and 98 percent of the people don't know who you are. You can go somewhere with your children without drawing special notice to yourself.

Being a celebrity puts everything out of whack for your children.

Long before he died, I thought the only way I could allow Scott to go his own way would be to shoot myself. The strain would be relieved, and he would be able to travel somewhere and possibly get rid of the affliction that was me and become a whole person.

He wouldn't have had to compete any longer because the competition would have ended.

***

I never saw my children as people because I was so disconnected from everything.

Even Joanne, who had been a wife, an actress, and a sex object to me until recently, has only recently become a person to me. And, little by little, my children have begun to develop as individuals.

***

I feel like someone who has been incarcerated and is suddenly released. He understands he only has five, six, or eight years remaining in his life, and that won't be enough time to make apologies. So he'll look at the unclimbed mountain and think to himself, "Well, I could've climbed that thirty years ago, or even just tried to attack it, but to try now with this little time and energy left is almost insurmountable."

Regardless, something will occur. The person will either be overjoyed at his newfound independence or suspect that the harm is so extensive that any dent that can be made will be minimal. One of them will triumph, and it would be presumptuous to think that you know which one it will be.

CHAPTER X

(Paul Newman made and distributed nearly twenty films during the 1960s. He garnered his first Oscar nomination of the new decade for his performance as Fast Eddie Felson in The Hustler, which he lost to Maximilian Schell for Judgment at Nuremberg, and his second two years later for Hud, which he lost to Sidney Poitier for Lilies of the Field. (Newman's co-stars Melvyn Douglas and Patricia Neal both won Oscars that night.) In 1967, he was nominated for another Oscar for Cool Hand Luke (together with costar George Kennedy, who won Best Supporting Actor). He ended the decade with Butch Cassidy and the Sundance Kid, one of the most commercially successful films ever, which was nominated for Best Picture (but lost to Midnight Cowboy). He had eleven Oscar nominations in his career, finally winning in 1987 for The Color of Money.

In 1968, he was nominated for Best Picture as the producer of his debut film, Rachel, Rachel, a passion project that received four nods, including Best Actress for its star, Joanne Woodward.0

Dede Allen

As I was wrapping up Bonnie and Clyde, Paul called and begged to see me about Rachel, Rachel (which was then titled "A Jest of God"). When I read the script, I was exhausted; Bonnie and Clyde was a thrilling but exhausting event. "Never again!" you exclaim after having a child.

Something about Rachel, Rachel made me very uneasy—perhaps it had something to do with things I was uncomfortable with. In Beverly Hills, I met with Paul and told him, "I don't like this—I don't think it's the right thing for me to do."

"That's precisely why I want you to do it," he said. "Joanne does not disagree with you about a lot of this, and that's why I want you-I want different points of view." One of Paul's major gifts was his ability to go straight for the truth.

Paul stated that he intended to direct the picture, which was critical to its production since it was "right for Joanne." Audiences, he claimed, were not receiving the full benefit of Joanne as an actor, so he decided to direct despite his reservations.

John Foreman

Paul considers Joanne to be a magical creature to which he must strive extremely hard to get near. As a result, he has had to put up with a lot from her throughout the years. She was as tough to direct in The Effect of Gamma Rays on Man-in-the-Moon Marigolds as I have ever seen a celebrity in all the years I have been in this profession. Finding that challenging woman was part of her professional process. Joanne had an intuition, which I had always suspected, that to be taken seriously as an actor, you had to be either prettier than everyone else or better, and she chose better.

Dede Allen

Nobody would have made a film like Rachel, Rachel-a film about a lonely thirty-seven-year-old woman who has never slept with a man? The studio agreed to let Paul create the film in exchange for an acting commitment from him. They also left us alone, which was the best thing that could have happened.

It was a watershed moment for me because it was not just one of my favourite films, but also one of my best job experiences. I believe the entire reason the picture worked was because it was loved into existence-no one was watching over us. The studio didn't give a damn. They couldn't care less about this insignificant effort. "Here's some film," they announced. "Go play."

On the first day of filming in Bethel, Connecticut, Paul addressed the entire crew, saying, "I'm a virgin." Please be patient with me. I need your assistance!" There was nothing the team wouldn't do to embrace Paul because he was so open and honest.

Stelle Parsons

I'd never rehearsed a film like that before, on a marked-out floor, like if it were a play. It was a lot of fun. It gave the film an extraordinary dimension. When we finally got to shoot the movie, it had nothing to do with what we prepared, but the characters had a certain heavy relaxation, a certain depth that was not conscious, that you couldn't act. I thought about how great Paul was to achieve that, because whether we wanted it or not, we had something that one does not generally see in a film.

Shirley Rich was a celebrated casting director for many Broadway shows and Hollywood films, including Rachel, Rachel.

When Paul made decisions, he would see things in someone-perhaps it was the actor in him. He could always discern the difference between what was good and what wasn't.

Actors recall Paul for making casting a pleasant experience. They didn't have to answer the question, "What have you done lately?" He always had their images and resumes, but whatever transpired during the reading was decisive.

His decisions are fantastic-he has a true feel of what is proper and excellent for what he is working on. He doesn't deliberate for weeks-

Paul never wastes time. That discipline extends to his acting as well.

Tom Cruise

I auditioned for Harry & Son mostly so that I could meet Paul. I was tense. When you're a young actor, you want people to enjoy you and your work, and you want to be accepted. The taps had been turned on, and I immediately thought of Risky Business. I entered the office. Joanne is knitting, and Newman is wearing a necklace with a beer can opener on it around his neck. He was dressed casually in an off-white pullover and pants. "Hey, killer," he remarked. "How are things going?" Very delighted to see an actor arrive, but also very relaxed.

We began filming a scene, and he was intrigued by my point of view and what I had come up with, and he was eager to explore it. I was really impressed. You imagine someone is one way, and then you meet him and discover that he can still be delighted by two actors performing a scenario.

Warren Cowan

My first memory of Rachel is reading the script on a plane to New York and then going to meet Paul at their apartment on Lexington Avenue the next day.

I recall them converting the apartment into a production office. People were working at two or three workstations in the entryway, and actresses were auditioning in the living room. Joanne had placed an ad in The New York Times the day before asking for a new nanny, so when the doorbell rang, they said, "Are you here for the movie or to apply for the nanny?"

Frank Corsaro was a renowned director of opera and theater, and an alumnus of the actors studio; he had a lead role in Rachel, Rachel.

In many ways, Paul's strongest performance as an actor was as the director of Rachel, Rachel. I've never seen such dexterity, and his incredible compassion shone through. He was able to channel some of his most vulnerable emotions through the characters in the picture.

Paul put very specific expectations on the cast as a director in areas of empathy and fun that were frequently lacking in his own work as an actor.

Dede Allen

Paul's affection for Joanne, not only as an actress but also as a woman, was so great that I believe it was really unsettling to him when things were heated, making the directing experience more difficult than it should have been. It must be terrifying to guide someone you care about and live with when there is conflict. Both were completely professional, although I recall Paul joking that "this directing situation is going to cost our marriage."

Stewart Stern

He didn't want to film the love scene by the sea when I was filming Rachel. He didn't want Joanne to be in that situation. His reasoning was, "Let's play it on her face later, when she remembers it."

He attended a rehearsal of it that night and walked away into the woods, and I followed him. He exclaimed, "No, no!" It's not going to happen. It's a personal preference! It's all about the actress!" I begged him to shoot it anyway. I repeated to myself, "You always have an option in the cutting room to throw it out, but this is not the time to make that kind of decision." I was practically in tears because I could feel the whole thing getting started.

Dede Allen

I recall that discussion: I recall working really hard to get those love scenes. I thought they were crucial-and it's strange because I don't recall ever testing the picture with that sequence out during the editing process. It was a beautiful, elegantly shot sequence, and I don't recall it ever not being cut.

Elia Kazan

Paul is a fantastic director; he's sympathetic, tough, and powerful. Rachel, Rachel, Rachel, Rachel was honourable, decent, and good. It would be difficult to withstand Paul's seduction. You'd do whatever he wanted, which is part of the director's role. It could perhaps be his strongest suit. Perhaps in five years, people will say, "Boy, Newman was a good actor, but when it comes to directing, he's better."

Dede Allen

I was never sure that Paul recognized how good he was, how talented he was, and how well he dealt with people, almost in the manner of someone who'd had years and years of managing groups of people. Kazan glides into a room like a master psychiatrist, knowing who you dump on and who you don't, when I'm vulnerable and when to send me roses. Kazan does it exceptionally well. I never had that feeling with Paul. I don't believe there is any deliberate manipulation.

Sidney Lumet was the director of the verdict.

I'm surprised Paul doesn't direct more because it appears to be a fantastic option for him. If you're worried about showing your vulnerability to the masses, it's obviously easier to limit the exposure to the very personal situations of players you'd get to know well during the directing process. It seems to accord with his talent and with my psychological impressions of him.

I had grown quite frustrated with Hollywood's studio structure by the time Cat on a Hot Tin Roof was released in 1958. At the time of Silver Chalice, I had signed a deal with Warner Bros. that gave them enormous control over what films I could do and how much money I could make from them.

John foreman

Warners began to loan him, which really irritated him because all of his great triumphs were on loan-out; they got approximately a hundred and fifty thousand dollars for him when he worked at MGM, and five to six hundred thousand dollars by the time he was at Fox. And he was still getting paid $2,000 every week.

Warner Bros. lied when they said they'd never compel me to make a film I didn't want to make. Finally, I dialled the studio's number. "Jack Warner," I introduced myself, "this is Paul Newman." "You go fuck yourself." It required the skill and bravery of my talent agency's head, MCA's Lew Wasserman, to find out how to calm things down and let me free-sort of. Lew called Jack Warner and recommended I pay half a million dollars to get out of their contract. I was terrified by the deal.

"Lew, this will make me an indentured servant for the next twenty years!"

"Let me worry about that," he said.

I was still scared, but the risk paid off in the end. I had repaid Warners $500,000 within a few years.

Jack Warner adhered to the "business is business" concept and made it clear that he harboured no grudges. But not long after that, he was in New York and saw one of my performances of Sweet Bird of Youth; he stopped by after the concert to say hello. I wouldn't let him backstage.

I was resolved to make my own decisions-to choose which projects to work on based on whether I truly wanted to work on them.

Robert J. Wagner played Paul's rival, the ruthless competing race car driver, in winning, and with Paul's help was cast in a key role in harper.

Paul was always dissatisfied with the studio contract system and the types of films they desired. That irritated him. He was always striving for more, for the edge, for values greater than what was expected of him.

As an actor, his cognitive processes were both perplexing and thrilling. When Paul considered a role or a character, his interests were so unusual that his depth of inquiry into life and behaviour was always far greater than mine. I'd never met somebody who worked so hard to reach where he is and to have the strength he does.

It's certainly no surprise that my political knowledge and participation increased as I reached the 1960s.

Perhaps it all started with Gore Vidal. We first met in 1955, when I was cast as the lead in his film The Death of Billy the Kid. Gore and his companion, Howard Austen, hosted a great celebratory meal for

Joanne and me during our honeymoon in Europe; when we returned to LA, we actually shared a rented property with them for a time.

We became fast friends, and whenever we returned east, we'd stay at Gore's country estate, Edgewater, near Red Hook, New York. Gore hosted a true salon there, with literary types, theatre people, and even some military personnel in attendance. Also, a number of political individuals, as Gore was both politically astute and engaged. We'd remain up late drinking copious amounts of booze, wine, and beer. Whether he went to bed at four a.m. or nine a.m., Gore was always at his typewriter working. I was always worried that I was difficult to talk to since I wasn't as well educated as Gore and his guests.

Of course, Gore comes from a prominent family; his grandpa was a US senator, and he grew up in Washington, DC. In 1960, Gore secured the Democratic nomination for Congress, earning the support of Eleanor Roosevelt for the Hudson Valley House seat long held by Republicans. Joanne and I were struck by Gore's liberalism and promised to assist. I made numerous trips to Gore's upstate New York district to campaign for him during my first political experience. We went door-to-door, and I delivered speeches in his honour. Gore eventually lost the election, but it was the start of my long-term involvement with Democratic politicians, which is maybe odd for an "emotional Republican" from Shaker Heights.

Marlon Brando called me about three years later, at the height of the civil rights movement and a burgeoning resistance to Governor George Wallace's rabid racism in the South, and asked if I would accompany him to Gadsden, Alabama, to help bring attention to and mediate a confrontation between the Black community and the town's big white-run steel makers. Tensions were high, and no conversations had taken place between Gadsden's white business class and the Black population.

Marlon had also requested Tony Franciosa and Virgil Frye, a boxer and actor, to fly down with him. So we did, and soon after landing near Birmingham, we noticed that our airport vans were being followed. We were being followed, and the individuals who were accompanying us forced us to transfer cars for our own safety. I don't believe there was any real physical danger, but we certainly didn't make many friends down there.

While we gathered with members of the African-American religious community, at least one business leader and Gadsden's mayor, Lesley Gilliland, refused to even acknowledge our presence. "They serve no purpose in Gadsden other than to cause trouble and chaos," stated the mayor of our group.

We went to numerous Black churches, shook hands with the parishioners, and asked for ideas on who we should meet and what we should say to help them with their voting rights and employment concerns. We were all staying at a hotel managed by one of the local clergy for two or three days. I was conversing with one of the Black activists who was also stationed there, and he was informing me about the police and troopers' brutal techniques against the protestors.

"Would you like to see what we get on a regular basis?" he inquired.

I told him I was curious, and he brought over a cattle prod used by cops on black people. I stated that I was curious to see how it felt. He then put it to the muscle that goes down my backbone, and I jumped approximately 10 feet across the room. It gave me a huge jolt, and all I could think about was what would happen if someone was shocked in the chest or stomach.

I'm not sure if there were any tangible outcomes from our trip, but we tried our best to reassure the community that they had our and our colleagues' support. The most crucial aspect, however, was the national media coverage we received. As a result of the wire photos and reports, several Southern theatre owners opted to take my movie off their screens.

By 1964, the national Democratic Party had invited me to its presidential convention in Atlantic City. Despite the fact that LBJ was extremely popular and had no genuine competition for the nomination, they wanted me to address the Young Democrats, energise them for the general election, and allay any concerns they had about LBJ's foreign policy. I was led into a massive auditorium filled with thousands of people, and my topic was the simmering war in Vietnam. Johnson's approach, which was quite effective, was that he would limit our participation in Southeast Asia, whereas his Republican opponent, Arizona's conservative Senator Barry Goldwater, would extend the US presence. I gladly—and regrettably in retrospect—gave my speech in support of his stated goals.

Years later, when the Pentagon Papers were released, it was evident that the White House had already decided to intensify the war in May 1964. As a member of the Armed Services Committee, Goldwater would have been aware of the decision—but couldn't say anything because it was a matter of national security. So there were two men with intentions to escalate in Vietnam, but only one admitted to wanting to do so, while the incumbent said he had no such plans. "Look, on this issue, it's going to be the same no matter who is elected—don't think for a minute that won't be the case!" Goldwater couldn't say.

I'd always suspected that there was some sleaze in government, but I'd never envisioned a president of the United States actually getting up and lying to the people. They were actively urging me to jeopardise my position and reputation in order to back someone who had already sunk us.

It was an awful feeling to know just how far LBJ had brought us all. I did everything I could to repair the damage four years later, at the next national election.

Harold Willens was a cofounder of the centre for defence information and a major supporter of progressive causes, including the antiwar movement and nuclear disarmament. He recruited Newman to donate and participate in these and other causes.

Paul was and has always been someone who made no pretence of knowing more than he did or being more profound than he is. He has always been modest about himself. But there was a willingness, almost eagerness, to learn, and this has continued for the entire time I've known him.

It was difficult to find a candidate willing to challenge his own party's incumbent president in a primary. While many on the Left urged some well-known antiwar national leaders to challenge LBJ and put an end to the Vietnam lunacy, only Senator Gene McCarthy, Democrat of Minnesota, rose to the occasion. McCarthy was barely unknown when he began campaigning as the antiwar candidate against Johnson in early 1968. He could walk through his hotel lobby in New Hampshire, the scene of the first fight, and not turn a single head.

I'd been in New York working on my film Rachel, Rachel, so I had a lot of time on my hands. I'd work on the film three days a week and then campaign for McCarthy in New Hampshire the rest of the time.

I'd never met the man before volunteering. But when we finally met for lunch, I discovered him to be a man of immense political and intellectual appeal. He was a razor-sharp senator with unwavering honesty. There was a running joke that if McCarthy were elected, he'd hang diplomatic pouches from the wall while penning poetry in a corner. I ended up spending the next forty-five or fifty days on the campaign trail doing everything I could to assist McCarthy defeat the president.

At first, I was strictly a grassroots activist, canvassing and speaking at Rotary and Kiwanis clubs, churches, high schools, and even from the back of some flatbed trucks. McCarthy was frequently present, and I'd introduce him, but there were times when I had to hold the fort because he was late. I was somewhat well prepared, well-read on Vietnam, and improved as I went along (as with everything else in life). Though we lost New Hampshire, the entire country was taken aback by LBJ's razor-thin victory—50 percent to 42 percent.

I then went to Wisconsin to assist McCarthy's campaign there. We could feel the momentum shifting McCarthy's way after a few days on the campaign trail; one late poll showed us up by more than fifteen points. When I returned to New York just before the election, I switched on my car radio to hear Lyndon Johnson say, "I shall not seek and will not accept the nomination of my party for another term as your president."

I was furious because Johnson refused to let us lick him. Of course, Bobby Kennedy chose to enter the race, which I thought was not cricket. McCarthy was my choice.

A few months later, when campaigning in Chicago ahead of the Illinois primary, McCarthy had to abruptly withdraw from an event, leaving me to the wolves. The event was set to take place in a poor Black area, and I was on my own in front of a large crowd. With the horror and pain of Bobby Kennedy's assassination just a week earlier, minority voters were suddenly giving McCarthy a second look, and as his surrogate, I was asked about race relations, equal opportunity, and other issues. It ultimately came down to one question, which someone in the audience asked: "What are you going to do for us?"

"Let me be clear," I added on the fly. "As long as the Vietnam War continues, there will be nothing for the Black community." Only by ending the war will the government have the energy and resources to address racial equality. But if we stay in Vietnam, you will receive nothing."

I honestly didn't know what else to say, but my response terrified me. It had just appeared in my mouth as I stood in front of the throng, and saying it out loud was thrilling.

The event I remember most vividly from that campaign occurred when I arrived late one night in one of the midwestern primary states, and the young campaign volunteer who welcomed me at the airport asked if I could boost the mood of the young campaign volunteers who were working their buttocks off for McCarthy. Despite the fact that it was already eleven p.m., I promised to walk over, say hello, clap them on the back, and provide some words of encouragement. When we got in the church basement office, there were still approximately a half-dozen people working—and a strange whiff of marijuana wafting through the air. I thanked everyone and started talking to one young man, maybe nineteen, with a beard and long bushy hair.

"Are you all college students?" I inquired. "Yeah," he said. "And where were you going to school?". "Princeton". "And you gave up a whole semester of Princeton to volunteer in McCarthy's campaign?". "Yeah, that's what I'm giving up". "And what do you get out of it?". "I want to be known as a revolutionary". "A revolutionary," I called him. "What's the benefit of being a revolutionary?". "Revolutionaries," he said, "get laid a lot."

So much for democracy's delight.

Harold Willens

106

When Paul spent weekends in New Hampshire campaigning for McCarthy in 1968, a rental firm made a nice automobile available to him. Paul learnt that Richard Nixon was visiting the state to campaign and would be using the same automobile.

"You'll find this car very suitable for you," Paul wrote and left in the car for Nixon. It has a bent clutch."

My overall impression of Paul is that he is the quintessential citizen who pays a high price in terms of much more than money for the things he values.

He is concerned with issues that are broader than himself. Macrocosmic issues affect him and elicit a response from him.

He also has the ability to understand that human endeavour, whether it's directing a film or saving the globe from extinction, necessitates a process, a process that shouldn't be assessed in terms of "Will the ten thousand dollars I contribute bring some specific result by next Monday?"

To my surprise and delight, this guy turned out to be acutely aware that history is a stream of events that comes before and follows us. He recognizes the importance of doing anything that can help steer the process in the proper direction.

George Roy hill and Stewart Stern

By the mid-1960s, Gore and Howard had relocated to Italy full-time. Long-distance relationships can be difficult to sustain, so when Gore invited Joanne and me to join him on a sailing voyage around Greece, it sounded like a fantastic opportunity to get away from our hectic lives and reconnect with one of our longstanding friends.

Gore had rented a four-stateroom launch (with crew), and we were to set sail from Piraeus in May, which is traditionally thought to be the ideal month for visiting the Greek islands of the Adriatic. If you're travelling past historical or political landmarks, there's no one better to travel with than Gore; he's a walking encyclopaedia, and for an illiterate like me, it's like having your own 24-hour tour guide. Even so, things got off to a bad start.

I misplaced my passport on the day Joanne and I flew into Athens. For a temporary replacement, all the embassy could do was hand me a slip of paper identifying me (in Greek) as Paul Newman, US Citizen. When we finally got our baggage to Gore's yacht, we met the captain and first mate—and made some disturbing findings. While we were aware that the captain was Greek, we were informed that his first mate spoke French and could talk with any of us and function as our liaison to the captain. The problem was that this mate couldn't speak a word of French and didn't even know what potage meant. "Well, there's going to be trouble," I thought.

Aside from our captain's language problems, he also made us nervous by knocking into things as we left the port. We literally bounced off the other vessels. Whatever direction we were headed, the captain was looking the other way, alertly and forcefully. (In some ways, the captain reminded me of myself: wherever there was knowledge, experience, or understanding and you had to put yourself in that direction to accept all that good stuff, I looked in the opposite direction.)

We also encountered what was considered to be the worst May weather in the Adriatic in fifty years within a day of leaving. Joanne had hung one of her Gucci dresses on the top bunk in our stateroom, and the ship's maid had failed to tie down the porthole as the rain began to fall; the water surged right through and was sucked up into the dress, which now resembled a child's bathing suit.

When we arrived at the first island on our schedule, our captain was unable to dock our boat because another 65-foot launch was obstructing our path to the harbour; he was at a loss for what to do. We all wanted to go into town and explore, but the only way to get there was in a three-person dinghy. (A Boston Whaler was attached to our ship, but its engine, of course, conked out.) So a mate rowed two of us in, then turned around and shuttled the other two of us in. We ate the best fish possible before being rowed back the same way we came. But the next morning, with the weather getting worse, our skipper thought it was too unsafe to continue sailing, so we had the mate row us back to shore. We strolled all around this lovely tiny island, and on our way back to the pier, we stopped to grab some bread, sliced meat, vegetables, and other necessities.

By this point, news must have spread that an American movie star was aboard this launch, which was anchored just three hundred feet from the dock. As we prepared to reboard our dinghy, fifty or sixty people gathered at the water's edge, watching us with interest. I jumped into the dinghy with our leeks, lettuce, and bread, while Howard immediately followed, hopping down on the outer gunnel— and toppling over the rowboat. The natives applauded politely as I emerged, saying "El comandante!" and "Il capitano!" and "Bravo!" and "Ole!" or whatever. So, in addition to my embarrassment, we were out of bread and leeks. But I have to say, that was hilarious.

We were once again wallowing in a turbulent sea as we set sail the next morning. Joanne was sitting on the deck, atop a large sea chest that had become free and skidded across the deck. Joanne was riding it like a colt until she crashed into the gunnel. It's remarkable she didn't overdo it.

"Get me off this fucking boat!" Joanne exclaimed in her finest Southern drawl.

We were able to convince the skipper to tack south and get the wind at our backs. He took us into the lee of another little island, when we heard gunshots and saw another yacht speeding at us, armed with a crew.

I was afraid we were being kidnapped. I advised Joanne to go downstairs and lock herself in the bathroom because Gore was sleeping below. I was wearing only a pair of shorts and no weapons, and when the boat approached, two young kids with submachine guns jumped onto it and pointed their guns at us.

The skipper of the second boat then got onboard and demanded everyone's papers. The skipper looked up at me, then back to the document, then back at us all when he got to the scribbled temporary passport I'd obtained from the American embassy. He signalled for the shooters to exit the boat swiftly, but warned that we would be following their watercraft for the next three or four hours.

Greece was, it turned out, in the midst of a coup, and our moron captain had sailed us into the lee of the small island where all the political prisoners were being held. Our captain was carried away for questioning when we followed their vessel to a different port. Joanne took a peek around the harbour and asked a local cop about the enormous boat that had just docked at the next wharf. "That's a ferry to Athens," he explained.

Joanne packed in under four minutes. She bought a ticket and dashed aboard the ferry, sobbing profusely. "I'll see you later, guys," she said as she left.

She travelled directly back to the United States from Athens, and I wasn't far after.

CHAPTER XI

(Paul Newman co-starred in the 1969 picture Winning with Joanne Woodward and Robert Wagner. It would spark a serious interest in motor racing in him that would last the rest of his life. He advanced to the point where he won his final race at Lime Rock Park in September 2007.)

I believe the IRS has audited me every year since 1972, and the main point of argument is whether my motor racing is a vocation or an avocation. Irving Axelrod (also known as Irving the Ax) , my lifelong lawyer, had to go down to the IRS on numerous occasions to make the point that it was anything but a hobby for me.

"You don't understand the psychology of racing," Irving pointed out. "Mr. Newman's career had struck rock bottom. He was a street person. And his battlefield management plan organisation determined that he needed to improve his image. At that moment, Mr. Newman and his management team agreed that he should pursue motor racing and become one of those macho people who get behind the wheel and risk their lives. So he tried it, and it worked.Many publications are now featuring Mr. Newman on their top pages. He rose to prominence as a racer, winning four national championships. He was this old man in a young man's sport, and he got a lot of mileage out of it."

However, this did not persuade the IRS that it was an accurate portrayal. So Irving supplied another important piece of evidence.

"You know those enormous seat belts that race vehicles use? Those are there to prevent Mr. Newman from exiting the car at any cost. Even if he urgently tries to claw his way out, the reason he's strapped in is so he can't escape." And I suppose they eventually bought it to some extent.

Jim "Fitzy" Fitzgerald was a champion auto racer and member of the newman-sharp racing team.

Paul and I met in 1972 at Road Atlanta. Paul was racing in a Datsun 510, and I was requested to show him around the circuit. I drove him around in a Nissan 240B, going around and around. He couldn't get enough of it. "Show me more," he insisted. "Do it again!" And when we were finished, he asked, "Do you have a cooler?"

"Oddly enough, yeah."

"Well, if you have the cooler, I have the beer."

We ended up staying at the Holiday Inn across from the track, which had linked rooms, for ten days. When we got home from the track, we'd crack open the beers, cook some popcorn, and gather some newspapers to hide the smell from coming out from under the door. Finally, Paul stated that he would have to call it a night in order to conduct some script study.

But, as luck would have it, it wasn't long until I heard a scratching noise on my door. Paul is the one.

"Fuck the script, study." Let's get started!"

So there was the beginning of the development of our friendship.

Paul and I grabbed a couple of beers, ate dinner, and then strolled around our motel the night before one of our races at the Mid-Ohio circuit. Because he wanted to walk arm in arm, you could tell what kind of mood he was in. "You're a pretty lucky guy," Paul told me. "Everybody likes you."

"Well, I'm not sure about everybody, but I do get along with folks."

"There are people who wouldn't mind putting a spear right through me," he remarked. "Most people don't like me."

I told him he was full of garbage, but he wouldn't listen. I wondered whether this is why Paul isn't more extroverted. Is this why he never lets anyone get too close to him? I know we all go through melancholy phases, thinking the world doesn't like us, but Jesus! Is Paul truly feeling this way?

I would frequently stay at his Westport home and spend a lot of time with his family. I'd tease him about Joanne, how lucky he was to have her.

"She isn't always perfect. We've got our issues. It hasn't all been peaches and cream."

Again, Paul was content to stop there.

Getting a clear tale has been tough for me since I was a child, and it continues to be challenging. I've always been suspicious.

My team competed in the 1986 SCCA runoffs in Atlanta, and I believe I qualified ahead of Fitzy by more than a second, and I had a twelve- or thirteen-second lead over him for the championship. But my automobile just lugged out of the seven turns. I was losing second gear and couldn't get it to hold. Fitzy continued to consume my lead. We exited the five, and he stayed right on my tail, but he didn't go around me. I knew he had me, but he didn't let me go. As I approached the straightaway, I recognized and thought to myself, "That fucker has instructions."

If someone had simply said, "Hey, Paul, don't be concerned about the win. Fitzy will not beat you no matter what as long as your car is running." Then I'd have said, "OK, fine." I footed the bill for the squad. I would have responded, "Well, I'll take this." Because I had unqualified Fitzy and outlasted him, and this was simply a gear-box problem. I'm not going to like it, but I understand."

There were no guidelines. However, our staff believes that Paul is our flagship.

Following that, several in my family denied what happened, waffled, and even told me, "Well, you could have just pulled ahead." "No," I replied, "I couldn't even shift the fucking car."

Fitzy was an excellent driver, the most successful in SCCA history, a member of my racing squad, and one of my closest friends. And, while no one pays much heed to superstition these days, Fitzy ordered a glass of sambuca to go with his after-dinner coffee the night before his death. There were four coffee beans floating on top of the table when it arrived. The problem is that drinking sambuca with an even number of coffee beans is considered unlucky. It's like trying to walk beneath a ladder.

In 1987, we were at St. Petersburg for the final Trans Am SCCA event of the season. Fitzy was the circuit's oldest racer at 65 years old. His mood was joyful the next day, at the time of the race.

I saw the accident. It occurred on the third lap. He'd run into a wall. There was no fire, and there was no damage severe enough to give a driver a headache. He should have been able to walk away from the car. So when one of the crew members walked over to the pit and informed us that Fitzy had been injured, that an ambulance was on its way, and that we should all rush over to the wreck, I had no idea what was going on.

"I'm not sure he wasn't hurt before he hit the wall," one of our team members told me, "because his head seemed down."

"What do you mean?" "When I saw him come around that last turn, his head was slumping forward." Fitzy wasn't moving, according to another crew member, and things weren't looking good. He wasn't alive when he arrived at the hospital.

All I could think was that Fitzy must have had a stroke when he came around that last corner. He was then reduced to the status of a passenger in a car. He provided no resistance to the crash and fractured his neck because his body would have been limp when he hit the wall.

Of course, the race had come to an end. There was a lot of debate over what to do, especially among my team. Everyone in the car, including myself, was waiting for a decision. Our team tried to pull the car off the track when the officials chose to restart.

"I don't think that's what Fitzy would have wanted," they said to me. "He'd want me to finish this race."

At that point, you can feel a variety of emotions, including rage and anger. When you're upset, you can actually drive very well if you don't make any mistakes. But when the racers were ready to go again, I couldn't start my car. I must have done something stupid by leaving one fuel pump on when I thought I had turned everything off, causing one of the cylinders to overflow with gasoline.

The humiliation of being unable to start the car! We attempted to push it, but it simply locked up. To the audience, I must have appeared to be doing some sort of act.

Fitzy embodied everything I love about racing. He had a strong assault in a car that I admired, and he provided the kind of camaraderie that racing should be about. It's not only about the engine and the speed; it's not a business or a career for me. It pulls me away from the characters in films, outside of the fictitious experience, into something genuine and extremely basic. And that speaks to whatever competitiveness I have as an actor, which I can't afford.

Fitzy was the greatest of the bunch because he broke past my stoic reserve. He was quite open and gregarious, and he frequently laughed. He was the fun side of racing, and we were good friends.

When I won the President's Cup, the greatest honour the SCCA bestows on its drivers, I had two key races almost back-to-back. In the first, I began out cautiously and was involved in a shoving mishap for which I probably held a lot of responsibility. It wasn't a particularly exciting race. I came in third place. I was embarrassed by my performance.

But in the following one, I just flew away. I was beating everyone by a second every lap, and no one could catch me. I won by a massive margin. It was a fantastic race. The problem is that as a racer, you can't have just one fantastic race. That is what distinguishes great racers from novices. Mario Andretti, who later joined my squad, never has a terrible race. He may have races where the car doesn't work or a tire blows out, but he never says, "Oh god, I drove badly." The excellent driver's perfection is always present and may be called upon on any given day. Someone like me has had some really good days as well as some really horrible ones.

It's never an issue of being irritated or losing your cool. The finest races for me, and many other racers, are the ones where you spin off early, lose your place, and have to go back and painstakingly knock off the other guys one by one. There's nothing to lose, nothing to gain, and nothing to safeguard at that moment. Everything gets amusing. Your mind is free, and your muscles are relaxed. You simply don't give a damn.

I should say that I own the best racing team in the United States. Mario is the most prominent, respected, and legendary racer of all time. But, while I always thought owning a team would be more rewarding than driving, it's just not the same as being in the car yourself.

Paul and I shared a room at the Indianapolis Athletic Club while filming Winning. We were learning race car driving together; he loved it and couldn't get enough of it. He'd be driving all day on the track.

I couldn't wait to get out of those vehicles. The damned things scared me, really scared me. I was happy to do it for the film, but I didn't want to be involved again. Paul was feeling something and gaining something from it. I said to myself, "Here's a man whose livelihood is himself and he's putting that at such great risk." He's out there-and he's pushed himself a little more each day. I'm not sure if it was some type of leveller for him, a way of dealing with death-related ideas that he never discussed. It's always "the car" or "the element" or "the fuel" or "the mistake" for these racers-they never say death. Yet it can happen in a split second due to someone else's error, a mechanical breakdown, or something else over which you have no control.

It looked like a crazy thing to do, but if you told Paul, "Don't drive," he'd just do it more. He didn't race to become a better man; it was all about the speed, the risk, and all that. He could feel it, although I couldn't.

Just as it started to rain, I jumped into one of our stock cars for some practice laps. It started to rain heavier as I was going around, and I wasn't paying attention, so I wasn't slowing down like I usually do coming out of a turn. "Boy, it's really coming down now, isn't it?" I realised. And when I enter the following corner, I exclaim, "Oops!" since the automobile does nothing. When I steer, there is no change in direction at all! I'm looking at a fence the next thing I know. I shattered a couple of ribs.

On the track, there's a great expression: "What's the most terrifying sound a driver can hear when racing a car?" The sound of his own voice saying "Oh, shit!"

George Roy hill

Paul seeks to challenge himself. He wants to be alive, and the only way to do so is to resist death-literally in the racing, and metaphorically in his profession.

James Goldstone was hired by Universal in 1968 to direct winning, about two rival Indy 500 drivers; he later directed Paul in When time ran out..., a big-budget disaster film.

I'd put fourteen to eighteen vehicles on the circuit with Paul when I was filming the racing scenes for Winning. All of our manoeuvres would be planned ahead of time, and I would signal Paul with flags—one flag would mean pass the guy on the right, another flag might mean pass the guy on the left, and so on. It was all very nicely coordinated, but with the exception of a couple of respectable adults, we were dealing with a bunch of ding-a-ling kids who drove their automobiles at breakneck speeds. And Paul was falling in love with speed and the personal challenge of finishing first.

For one phase of the race, I needed a series of photos of all the cars passing Paul, so we started with Paul in first place and all the kids behind him. By the time I got my footage from the camera car, Paul was right where the script indicated he should be: last. So I raised a green flag to indicate that the shot was complete, and Paul stepped right into it. They were driving with a huge star, and they had been told, "We can't kill him—he's an amateur, and you're pros."

But Paul kept going faster, overtaking each of those cars, and our safety man was hollering at me, "I'm gonna put on the light to get them off the track—everyone's driving too fast." Paul rolled into the pits in second place, having passed fourteen other drivers. He had the cutest embarrassed expression on his face. He knew he shouldn't have done it, but he felt good—just like a kid.

Perhaps he was demonstrating that it wasn't about how much you were paid or whether you won an Academy Award, but about who was in charge and who had balls.

And now I'll let the world in on a little secret.

I needed a few more inserts to go into a montage of simply Paul's eyes inside his racing goggles after I finished the photo and was putting it together. Though I got very fantastic close-ups of Paul driving at 120 mph, I only needed forty seconds of the bridge of his nose and his eyes.

The issue was that Paul couldn't fly from Connecticut to Los Angeles right away. But then I had an idea: why not use Paul's brother, Arthur, as our production manager for the shot? During the shoot, I'd grown to know Arthur very well. I summoned him to my office, where we fitted him with Paul's goggles. "Yeah, I think we can get away with that; we don't have to wait for Paul."

So we shot his eyes, and they received maybe three cuts in the end. But in Winning, those are Arthur Newman's eyes, not Paul Newman's famed blue eyes. The brothers don't resemble each other, but they share the same eyes. We were successful.

Michael Brockman

"You want to do something?" Newman asked me before I started acting class. "Go make a scene for me." So I get a copy of Sweet Bird of Youth and go over the monologue in which Paul's character reflects on his youth.

We were packing up after an event at the Orange County International track when Paul asked me to climb in a race vehicle and drive down the straightaway. We rush out, and Paul tells us, "Do the scene." So I deliver the speech at the end of the Orange County straightaway, rigid as a board.

Paul laughs and says, "Too much Beethoven, not enough Stravinsky." I recognized Beethoven, but not the other person, so Paul continued. "You're all in the same key—bring some life into it." Do whatever makes you happy. Simply be yourself. Such as this!"

And then he cuts fifteen lines from the monologue. He hadn't done it in over a decade. It was wonderful, so real, so convincing. Then he came to a halt and remarked, "Or, you could try it this way." And then, all of a sudden, he takes a 180-degree turn. Then he goes through three more iterations. Everyone is gathered at the end of the drag strip. I couldn't believe it, and thinking about it still gives me chills. He's been that kind of friend to me.

John foreman

Elizabeth Taylor and Richard Burton were the first performers to be paid a million dollars for a single film. I was always proud that Paul was the third child. That's what I got him as a prize for Winning.

I was up at the Portland International Speedway when John Huston called. He'd recently directed me in The Life and Times of Judge Roy Bean, one of my favourite films. He was one of maybe a half-dozen persons I've known with whom I wish I'd felt more at ease; I regret it. I could always communicate things with him in a creative way, but I wasn't loose or natural enough to be socially enjoyable for him; we'd run out of things to say.

Anyway, I answer the phone in my hotel room in Portland and am delighted to hear John's voice.

"Are you racing this weekend?" I'm coming to pay you a visit!"

"That'll be wonderful, John, but it's a pretty long trip up here."

"Where are you?" he inquired.

"Well, you dialled, don't you know?"

"My girl did that," he said. "Now, where are you?"

I told him, and he said, "I'll be right there."

And he boarded an aircraft in Los Angeles and flew up from California.

On a Saturday, as I was driving this monster Datsun with almost 900 horsepower, John arrived. The automobiles took his breath away.

He ended up not staying for the entire race on Sunday.

"Take good care of yourself, kid," he advised. He then boarded his jet and took off.

CHAPTER XII

It's an interesting test to see how far you can go with the drinking without completely self-destructing. In the early 1970s, I believe I took it as far as it could go before understanding it. It was similar to climbing Mount Everest in that you could say, "Okay, I've done that-now let's quit and move on to something else."

When I didn't overdo it on the alcohol, it seemed to help me focus a lot better. According to what I've read about Jackson Pollock, he may have been the same way. The first four drinks would open a window for him with folks who were otherwise unable to communicate with-for around twenty minutes. He'd have some meaningful and intriguing things to say about art and himself by his sixth beer. But by then, the window had closed and remained closed.

There was a time when alcohol enabled me to do things I couldn't have done otherwise. It was the key, but not necessarily the key to the room. It allowed me to think about things in the solitude of the restroom or basement. Things I couldn't otherwise release and wouldn't have recognized or seen.

When I was younger and did a lot of television, I'd book a room at the old Emerson Hotel and shut myself inside with a screenplay. I don't mean I'd go on a four-day drunken adventure. I'd sit there, work on the script, scribble notes to myself, then have a beer around dinnertime. Then I'd have two more drinks, then five beers, while cutting, editing, and making notes to myself.

I'd wake up the next morning and realise that 95 percent of the notes I'd made were bad, so I scratched them out so no one could ever read them. They were basically drunken crabs. But 5% were physicalizations, mannerisms, and bits of stage business that may be interesting-and they all felt too out of the ordinary for me to think of in a regular condition.

Gore Vidal has always justified his addiction to alcohol on the basis of its artistic merits. And I know there are some mental breakthroughs that I was able to achieve that I could later apply onstage. For someone as controlled as I am, experiencing the thrill, the luxury, of being out of control, not knowing what's around the next curve, and continually putting oneself at danger, is just pleasant. There are dreadful, bad things that happen when you drink alcohol, as well as dangerous things. I'm surprised I made it through.

Tom Cruise

Paul is always injuring himself. He'll torment himself by drinking a case of beer and then spending hours in the sauna. He chuckles about it, saying that what alcohol does to your body and what a sauna does to your body are equivalent to continually pulling yourself from one extreme to the next. He's a combustible man, yet he keeps himself in check and manages himself. He appears to deal with his pain in a different way and is not as self-destructive as he formerly was. He has always sought out stabilising influences in his life, such as becoming an actor, Joanne, and sticking with those things.

Robert Webber

Paul compared his drinking to that of his character Brick in Cat on a Hot Tin Roof. He'd be drinking a particular amount, then suddenly, click, you'd turn off and forget. It's fascinating to go black and still function. My best friend was a devout Catholic who didn't follow the rules of the church. So he'd go out, black out, and do anything he wanted without feeling guilty since he couldn't remember anything. Does Paul agree with this? "This is as far as I want to go now," there's clearly a trigger at work. I'm turning, and I don't want anyone to know what I'm doing."

I recall Paul once abstaining from heavy liquor. "I drink only beer," he'd say. True, but he drank a case a day. We were at a party when I noticed that all of the booze was disappearing. I questioned how someone could drink so much: I'm not sure how long he kept it up. He was never a loud drinker. As I previously stated, he would simply click away.

Mort Sahl was a controversial political satirist and stand-up comedian who first befriended Paul in the mid-1950s.

How many movies have you watched in which Paul Newman enters in the morning and plunges his head into an ice-cold sink? I believe he completed it in thirty-eight photographs. Dreams are resilient.

Paul relished his long sauna sessions. We'd go into one, and he'd fill a large brandy snifter with ice cubes and Scotch. He would cry when he told me about his mother. She used to entice him. If she saw anything negative about him in the papers-say, a negative review-she'd clip it and mail it to him just to punish him.

Paul may feel depressed. "Why can't people be tolerant?" he would wonder. "Perhaps you can't get through the night without three bottles of Scotch." If somebody can get through the night with a snake, you should leave them alone-at least they survived."

Paul used to stay up all night drinking. I'm not sure what it was all about, unless it was about people not being up to the task. Every performer I've ever met assumed he was receiving a free pass. And I'm sure Paul thought he was stealing the money and was wondering when it would all catch up with him. People who are unhappy with themselves will go to any length to feel better. Philanthropy is intended to lift their spirits, but it only works for a few minutes at a time.

Of all, he had so much going for him-marriage, stardom-but even at work, there were always problems. Paul was always thought to be operating in the shadow of Marlon Brando, and even after he truly emerged, he never won an award. For a while, Steve McQueen worried him; he saw McQueen as the rise of the illiterate in acting. "You don't know how lucky you are," Paul would tell me. "All I get is applause, but you get respect."

Arthur Newman, Paul's older brother, was a production manager on many of his films.

Paul was a huge fan of Fredric March. "Arthur, you have to watch Paul on the drinking thing," Freddie told me when filming Hombre with Paul. I've seen more outstanding performers perish as a result of alcoholism than anything else."

Personally, I don't believe it hindered his work or that there was ever a day of poor performance as a result of his drinking. After a day of shooting, Paul would just return to his motel room and drink, but you never saw him getting drunk in the local bars.

I believe Paul's addiction to physical fitness and the sauna cooked some of that terrible crap out of him before it finished him. Alcohol kills nerve cells, and the cells of the nervous system do not regenerate. So, instead of destroying twenty-eight cells, the booze only killed thirteen in Paul.

Look, all humans are built with self-destruct devices. And individuals spend their entire lives attempting to press that button and self-destruct. Every time they press the button, it causes harm, which accumulates. The harm is small at first, but it impacts you later and grows more and larger.

That I was susceptible to addiction or alcoholism may have been better or worse for me. The fact that I could have drunk more reflects the reality that I couldn't be persuaded to do so. The fact that I could have drunk less indicates that I couldn't be persuaded to do so. Whatever level I pursue is like water seeking its own level. The individual seeks the point at which it can be convinced to be one of two things.

I suppose it's better that I didn't reach for a kilo of cocaine than that I did. That I didn't was singularly me-and evidently, to the chagrin of certain others, distinctively not them. They did, but I did not. There are some people who don't drink, don't use cocaine, and don't do anything else. That's all there is to it. I commend them. It's also not their mother, father, or uncle-it's always a combination of elements that make up someone.

What I know about nature and nurture is that they are split in some way based on the individual. However, what that individual accomplishes as a result of being inadequately reared or natured ultimately belongs to them. People must accept responsibility for their actions.

If I had to define "Newman" in a dictionary, I'd say it means "one who tries too hard." A huge part of me believes you're a free agent within your genetics. And saying that "Mommy never kissed me" is nonsense. But I had a pretty low view of myself, which had to come from somewhere.

Paul in the early 1960s

Joanne, too, would stay up late in the early years of their marriage. She'd eventually just get out of her chair, walk into their bedroom, and shut the door. That was the end of it. She simply couldn't be a part of it any longer.

Joanne Woodward

Paul almost killed himself in 1971 while directing Sometimes a Great Notion in Oregon. He rolled out of bed one night. I discovered him on the floor, bleeding from the head, and I came dangerously close to exclaiming, "This is it, I just can't stand it." Paul gave up hard booze after finishing that picture.

I used to believe that the only tranquillity Paul ever found was when he was dead drunk. He now finds it in race cars. Peace and grace, the assurance that he has done something worthwhile.

I was in a state of disarray while working on Sometimes a Great Notion. I was restless, and I was at odds with everyone. There were also some trying periods with Joanne. The film was being produced by the Newman-Foreman Company, I was starring, and our director, Richard Colla, had to be replaced. I ended up having to direct the film myself, and the production was abruptly halted because I was in a bad motorbike accident near our Oregon site. I was under too much pressure from all sides, and I didn't ask for it.

Despite being blasted, I thought I put in a lot of effort on this project. The booze contributed to your sense of accomplishment. Perhaps it was a naive sense of accomplishment.

George Roy hill

Paul called and asked if I could come to the Oregon set and assist him. He was stumbling. I boarded my plane and headed out there, where I spent about a week reviewing the film recorded by both Paul and Colla and working on the script. I believe my presence provided him with more psychological assistance than professional assistance, as well as some extra confidence.

When I first worked with Paul on Butch Cassidy, he'd just finished directing Rachel, Rachel, for which he won the New York Film Critics Award and was nominated for the Directors Guild Award. Though Paul never mentioned it, I knew I had to deal with it. But it seemed as if there was a gigantic billboard behind him that said, "I just won the director's award!"

He was always grateful that I came out to Oregon, though I think he got more out of it than I gave.

John Foreman

We moved straight from Sometimes a Great Idea to Judge Roy Bean. What made the difference for Paul? With John Huston directing, Paul didn't have to worry about both directing and ensuring the film's success. And in between those two images, Paul made the decision to stop drinking.

Joanne Woodward

Drinking used to be the source of our distress. He's drinking less and less these days. I told him a few weeks ago: "That tiny glass of wine you're now drinking is just a pacifier-it's not that you need it, it's just you're afraid to let it go."

Sydney Lummet was a prominent American director, best known for films such as 12 Angry Men, Serpico, Dog Day Afternoon, and The Verdict, starring Paul.

Paul and I were discussing the drinking habits of his character, Frank Galvin.

"I know about that," he admitted. I received the impression that Paul, too, had a problem at one point, but I never inquired more.

We talked about "playing the denial," which was one of acting coach Sanford Meisner's brilliant ideas. What is the best way to get drunk? As someone who declares, "I'm not drunk, I'm sober." You pretend to be sober and make every attempt to stay sober. Paul was preoccupied with self-pity since a drunk is, by definition, self-pitying. Paul was not going to burst into tears in his cups.

Paul devised these physicalizations, which, while uncomfortable, showed Galvin's condition. The first time we see him, he's heading to a funeral and spraying Binaca in his mouth; this was Paul's invention, as was Galvin's habit of putting eyedrops in his eyes.

Galvin had to remain moving to stay sober; immobility meant he'd lift a glass-when he's working, he has to stay in motion. You can see the resolution in Galvin/Paul's final presentation to the jury—he doesn't move at all.

I don't think I ever had a comfortable emotional moment in a film until The Verdict. In reality, I can only recall a couple of memorable scenes from my flicks.

Lumet hands you the script, you come in on a Monday morning, read it around the table, and then you begin blocking. It took me a long time to finish that character; I'd been behind with those long scenes with the judge and the jury. I returned home and concentrated on those lines.

Sidney Lumet

During The Verdict rehearsals, there was a pivotal moment. Paul had discreetly informed me that he preferred to start with a character's externals: How does the voice sound? What about the body? I don't care where the acting comes from; I'll work however an actor wants

129

to work.

At the end of our second week, we did a run-through; Paul still had the book in his hands, and he had only memorised about a third of the script. He gave a very decent performance, but it lacked life. I sent the cast home after making some comments to them, however I begged Paul to stay. "What's the matter?" I said in so many terms. It isn't working."

"Oh, Sidney, it's just the lines; I'm having so much trouble with the fucking lines." "Don't worry, I'll be fine."

"No way, Paul. It's not because of the lines."

He blinked quickly and asked, "What do you think the problem is?"

"I think you have to make a decision," that's what I said. "You have to determine how much of yourself you want us to see. The heartbeat is absent, not you."

Paul remained silent. We took a weekend off. He was a different actor when he arrived on Monday. It was all there, and there was little else to do after that. Paul, I believe, was waiting for someone to make a demand on his talent. He understands what good acting is, and good acting is about self-discovery.

I first encountered inebriated performers in the summer of 1948. And by "drunk," I mean both offstage and onstage. I'm not sure how I got through it.

As a first-time intern at the Priscilla Beach Theatre in Plymouth, Massachusetts, I had the distinction of stage-managing some plays. The theatre was known for doing a number of current shows for brief runs, often drawing large crowds with big-name Hollywood or Broadway performers taking the leads and interns doing the rest. We also took these productions on short excursions around Cape Cod.

The suspense drama Laura drew Diana Barrymore and her third husband, Robert Wilcox. Diana Barrymore was the daughter of the great John Barrymore, and Wilcox was a regular leading man, mostly in B movies. We were scheduled to perform at a theatre in Woods Hole on an unusually designed stage; as I stepped in, I thought we ought to do some sort of rehearsal before we went on. So, as an apprentice stage manager, I scheduled one for 4:00 p.m. on opening night. This was unprecedented for an inexperienced stage manager. And as soon as Diana and Bob walked in at four o'clock and saw the arrangement, they ran across the street to the bar and got drunk. They were just fractured when they returned near our eight o'clock curtain.

Diana had to make multiple crosses in front of a large sofa that was literally twelve inches or so from the apron; the crowd kept giggling because it looked like she was going to tumble into the house. They were fumbling their lines, and when one of the other performers (as per the script) shoved Diana into the sofa, the entire sofa collapsed backwards, exposing Diana's entire crotch to the audience. It was hilarious.

After one of the Woods Hole shows, another intern, Charlie North, and I were assigned to transport Bob and Diana back to their company-provided cottage, which was approximately a half-hour drive away. Charlie drove, and in the spirit of our passengers, we completed the journey in approximately eighteen minutes, ignoring stop signs and red lights and rolling over curbs. We'd actually purchased a case of beer to carry back to our neighbouring dorms; I believe we'd consumed most of it by the time we arrived. We reasoned that if we were going to get hit, we might as well all be rubbery at the time of impact.

The stars' cottage featured a large lamp in front that lit up the porch and made it visible from the female apprentices' dormitories. They began squabbling just as we were about to release Bob and Diana. As the argument heated up, Wilcox grabbed the front of her sundress and yelled, "How do you like that!" They were both screaming. And you could hear one window after another in the dorm finally slamming shut.

Things were once again identified for me by really hard work and extremely hard partying. And there's a twist....

Meade Roberts

I'd travelled to Philadelphia to see Paul, who was performing The Desperate Hours on a pre-Broadway tour. We had dinner at the Variety, an exclusive club for travelling showpeople in the Bellevue-Stratford Hotel. Diana Barrymore staggered in; it was probably 1955, and she was at the bottom of her career, schlepping around the country in a horrible French farce called Pyjama Tops. She was an alcoholic, obese beyond belief, and she was in the Pyjama Top play with her husband, Bob Wilcox, who was also an alcoholic.

"There's Diana Barrymore," Paul said quietly. He told me how he'd known her well enough at Cape Cod to say, "Good evening, Miss Barrymore."

"Do you think I should go over and pay my respects?"

"I'm sure she'd appreciate it." It's only been seven years since summer stock, and now you're the star of Desperate Hours, and she's doing some turkey."

So Paul stood up, walked over to her table, and said, "Miss Barrymore"-all he could say before she glanced up at him and shrieked, "Marlon! Marlon!" She grabbed Paul, pushed him backwards, and kissed him on the lips until Wilcox and another guy had to pull her away. Paul's face was the colour of a beet, and I'm sure she had no idea she'd ever met Paul Newman.

He returned to our table and said only one word: "Jesus."

When I went over to Diana's table, I noticed this little old face on this little old woman, who was probably in her thirties at the time. She was completely unrecognisable.

It was the same thing that happened not long after in Beverly Hills. When I came into La Scala, I heard a voice say, "Paul?" I looked about, but it was dark and I couldn't see anything. And when I heard "Paul?" again, I understood it was coming from someone sitting alone in a booth. I approached and couldn't place this wounded face with black-circled eyes.

"Paul, it's me-Pier Angeli," she said, and I was taken aback. Pier co-starred with me in The Silver Chalice (while she was dating Jimmy Dean, who was filming East of Eden in the opposite studio) and Somebody Up There Likes Me. It hadn't been all that long. And here she was, this once-attractive lady with a small gift but a tremendous sense of physical flair. Her head was the size of a pumpkin, with no distinguishing features or even a resemblance to what she had once looked like. It was horrifying and terrifying.

Diana and Pier both died at the age of forty. Wilcox made it to the age of forty-five.

CHAPTER XIII

I'm in the pool hall at the Hole in the Wall Gang Camp when this little child with beautiful pigtails walks over to me with the help of a walker. I take her up because one of the counsellors says she needs to go downstairs. I see that both of her legs are plastic as I carry her; I can feel the rivets against my arms. When I get her downstairs, I raise her up and ask, "Are you okay?"

"Yeah," she says, "I'm fine," and she walks away to play.

***

I've always doubted my altruistic instincts. I'm not sure how altruistic they are. Or how charitable, Christian, or anything else you want to call it. The only thing I can say in my defence is that I do things, which is preferable to not doing them.

I'm dubious of my philanthropy because I'm not sure which came first, the urge and then the theory or the theory and then the urge. The notion is, of course, that having the luck of the draw, living in a democracy, being of majority colour, having an opportunity for education, enjoying the Bill of Rights, the Four Freedoms, and everything else are all advantages. And that it must be seen as a privilege with the unstated obligation to extend a helping hand to those who have less than you.

But isn't it easy to be hypocritical in this situation? Would you say, "The greatest enjoyment I've had is when I've given back to the community even as I've taken from it" ? I obtained it first for myself, so I can afford to be charitable; I won't be financially impacted. What will happen to me if I give away 10 million dollars? That will not alter my way of life. I'm not going to eat any less well. I'm still capable of putting a Buick engine in a Volvo.

To be honest, the simplest thing I can do is give money out. It does not appear to be the kind of sacrifice that would increase the splendour of the gift. Is it true that I am a philanthropist, as many in the media have labelled me? A philanthropist, in my opinion, is someone who gives up a completely cushy way of life, goes out into the community, gets his hands dirty, and dedicates himself to whatever keeps them dirty. That person's grace is imposing.

Time is difficult to give. To provide less privileged people with hands-on relationships. That's one of the main reasons I doubt myself.

I recall taking bushel baskets of food and hand-me-downs to my aunt's church for Thanksgiving when I was a youngster; we were also given addresses of needy families for my mother to drive to and drop items off there, as well as at Christmas. There were children who lacked shoes. The poverty astounded me. It felt like a threat of future anguish, and it rendered me immobile. I'd grown up in a super sanitary household where anything unsterile or reeking of mustiness or decay was strictly forbidden.

I often feel that the source of my altruism sprang from having no civic instincts at all, inventing them like I did everything else. Newman the Football Player, Newman the Actor, Newman the Citizen, Newman the Lover-all of it was invented by Paul Newman. You can practise generosity just by believing that you lack it and that it is something you should have. You ladle it out of a pot like soup, but it's not anything you made. I'm quite worried about how things appear, and being charitable is a lovely thing to do. It's easy to be charitable if it doesn't cost you anything; it's not like the folks who go out and help people at the risk of their own lives.

My gut feeling? I'm conscious that it's in my nature to despise everything I do-despise work, despise friendship-until I can't tell the truth any longer. I weigh everything carefully, attempting to be fair to my motivations, myself, and everyone else. I put everything on a scale to make sure it doesn't tip over, because the second it looks like it may, I add something on the other side.

Stewart Stern

I used to be troubled by the mystery of what Paul thought of me, how he felt about me, since you could take a multiple-choice test to see what emotions were going on behind that quiet face, that silence. But then, while I was unwell, I overheard Dad discussing me in intensive care with the physicians. I recognized that his compassion lies beneath the stillness.

George Roy hill

If I ever become melancholy, he always calls to make sure I get out of the home and will take me out to dinner or anything. He isn't just calling me and asking, "How are you today?" "Meet me at Louie's for a drink," he says, and then we'll have dinner and then meet Joanne and go to the movies or something. In that regard, he is highly active. That has always been really important to me. I don't have any other pals who would go to such lengths to support me.

***

When things come too effortlessly, it appears that you are never fully aware of the impact they will have. It seems absurd that a salad dressing that began so frivolously might now earn $19 million each year. If the earnings are $3.5 million, which is certainly the biggest margin of any food firm in the US, I'd have to earn $3.5 million from my own investments and acting jobs to give that much away without being taxed. I can't give away more Newman's Own profits than the equivalent of 100% of my earnings. Unless I'm dead, in which case

I'll be able to give away more than I make.

The fact that the salad-dressing money goes to charity isn't really remarkable; it goes there because doing anything differently would have been tacky. The whole thing started as a joke when two old friends, A. E. Hotchner and I were having fun pouring homemade salad dressing into old wine bottles and selling it in Connecticut tea shops and the like. It simply took on a life of its own. The more people said, "This isn't going to work," the more determined I became to make it work, even if it meant putting my name and image on the labels, something I never thought I'd see in my life (certainly not with my blessing).

But seeing this little bottle running around looking for a home, bumping into closed doors, then turning around and looking for another path until the answer it found was charity, then finding a rich uncle who helped it find its own life without asking unexpected favours allowed me to say, "Why not?"

As I have stated, it is not surprising that the funds were donated to charity. That it can turn a profit of $6 million or $7 million per year while being completely pure and unadulterated-and that I don't syphon something off for myself-that's the surprise.

I know a number of people who have worked for charities, people who raise a lot of money-they do appearances, go on TV, whatever- and get paid enormous sums for their efforts. People believe they do it for free. They are not.

I'm not sure why I'm changing. I don't believe it has anything to do with the impending death; I don't understand the urge. I believe that beginning the camps in the mid-1980s had anything to do with it, because setting that up was as random as a shift in myself. It was simply an idea that came to me, along with the means to carry it out. There was a strong sense of serendipity in the air.

The death of my friend Bruce Falconer in 1987 was undoubtedly an inspiration. He was a Connecticut architect with a strong sense of humour. He had lost a leg in a childhood accident, but he continued to pursue boating in a way that almost got him on the Olympic squad; I recall him flying to Italy for the tryouts one year. When cancer took his life at the age of fifty-two, all I could think was, "What a tragedy!" But then I realised that if what happened to Bruce was a tragedy, what must it be like for eight-, ten-, or twelve-year-old cancer patients who don't even have the short chance at life that Bruce did? And shouldn't these youngsters have a chance to feel the same sense of accomplishment that Bruce did? Shouldn't these children be cared for in a way that allows them to succeed?

So I simply dove in. I may have questioned my motivations, but not what was to be done. It was an act that took on its own emotional life and compassion. I just got up one day and decided, "Well, that's what I'm going to do." Knowing that providence would take care of such a good concept, there was no way it wouldn't be finished. As a result, it was constructed. And became a significant source of inspiration for many individuals. And it inspires me as well.

Not that providence would have changed me, but imagine you've committed $14 million to a children's camp and only had $7 million on hand. Unless the salad-dressing firm went belly up, the biggest danger I faced was having to borrow money against my future profits. And even that danger vanishes when a young Saudi boy comes to Connecticut and you play Ping-Pong with him.

The child informs you that he has a potentially fatal blood illness and is now residing in Washington, D.C. And that he has ties to the Saudi royal family, whose crown prince is also their ambassador to the United States and lives in Washington. And, as a Muslim and a Saudi, the child has the authority to petition the king directly through the crown prince. Then you're travelling back to Connecticut from Washington, DC with a check for $5 million for the camp and a letter saying the money is a gift from the king and people of Saudi Arabia.

Who can explain this? Who knows how merely recognizing the courage of those camp kids and how they deal with their situations sparked an unknown and previously unresponsive mechanism in me? A system that allows me to peer into myself and see what might be lying there. So you just change? The answer could simply be, "It was time." Suddenly, here I am, an atheist, a nonmetal physicalist, smack dab in the heart of God.

It's strange. It's natural. It's also inexplicable.

I recently met an eight-year-old boy at camp who wasn't very mobile; his legs and hands were severely impaired. His own immune system had assaulted his body in some way, and now his body was rejecting itself. He was sitting on one of the large boulders near the camp entrance, talking about God with one of our counsellors. The youngster stated he didn't know much about God, but he did know about the big bang hypothesis, and he knew how much energy was expended in that concept, which he compared to an atomic bomb. But the boy stated he understood that you couldn't pull more energy out of something than was put into it.

"Well," the counsellor explained, "I think I get more energy back from camp than I put into it."

"Well, you see, maybe that's what God is," the eight-year-old responded back to the counsellor.

I consider how fortunate I have been to live so long that whatever I achieve after this is gravy, and it occurs to me that children who do not even have the beginning of that privilege before it is threatened deserve something. If you have the ability, you should do anything you can to provide them with an experience they will remember. What could be more significant?

The camp is about a personal drama as intense as any he has ever experienced. Sometimes people are completely congruent with themselves, when the impulse and the result are precisely in sync. That camp is the most authentic representation of him; it is who he is. Paul adores that camp, and the reality of their connection draws everyone in. It's incredible.

I made a lot of requests on behalf of the Hole in the Wall Gang Camp. You go out and do fourteen services. You've had your photo taken 6,000 times. You host dinners in Boston, Hartford, New Haven, and Stamford to generate funds. It was well worth it. I flew to St. Louis to see August Busch, who owned Budweiser at the time. "August, I want you to be in charge of our camp's crown jewel, the mess hall," I said as I strolled into his conference room.

"How much do you want?" he asked back.

"I need $866,000. And we'll back it up."

"Deal," he said, and I walked away. It took roughly eight minutes to complete.

After that, I wrote Busch a letter in which I congratulated him for being the first corporate donor to provide us with the kind of support we hoped for from the business sector. His was a lavish gift, I wrote, and I had given it much care. "In all the years since I was in the Navy, starting at the age of eighteen," I continued, "I've consumed approximately two hundred thousand cans of Budweiser beer." So, if you look closely at the numbers, your contribution amounts to roughly a four-dollar-per-bottle rebate. And since you've had the money since 1944, it's not all that much. Nonetheless, I am grateful."

***

I suppose it hasn't hurt that I'm a relatively soft touch most of the time, at least monetarily. I recently added everything up and learned that I was in charge of forty-two people. That may not seem like much to a General Motors executive, but to someone like me, it was horrifying. I couldn't just supervise the construction of forty cars and then sell them to recuperate my investment. Furthermore, I'll admit that only approximately half of the people on my payroll were serving a legitimate purpose.

Of course, it's tough to let go of so many people after you've been responsible for them. How did I eventually reduce the number of people? As a result, the good Lord let them go. Perhaps I felt forced to assist others in order to justify my own accomplishment.

That, I feel, has a substantial amount of truth. I felt that a lot of my success was based on how I looked rather than what I accomplished. I felt forced to give it away because I believed I had less reason to be proud of my accomplishments, that I deserved it less. That is no longer how I feel. For me, the camp and what happens there are as emotional as what is going on at home and with this narrative project. My insulation isn't quite there yet, but it's starting to deteriorate.

CHAPTER XIV

I believe you begin your life with a specific quantity and type of people with whom you are friendly. As you get older and more successful, you begin to make more friends for the wrong reasons. On the one hand, I hope I'm not as paranoid as my mother was, but on the other, I know there have been people who have taken advantage of our friendship to make me feel exploited, and I'm always leery of it.

I'm not sure what my old age will be like because I don't have many pals. It's difficult to feel lonely in New York, but I do. When Joanne is gone or I've been alone for a longer period of time than I'm used to, I realise there aren't many people I can rely on, and the ones I can rely on are few and far between. I wouldn't know who to call if I needed companionship. Because most of the people I know are not here, I simply go about the home and bump into objects. I'm not sure I'd have it any other way, because I don't seem too concerned about it; so it can't be all bad. Or perhaps I'm simply too proud to be seen putting in the effort.

Mrs. Joanne Woodward

It takes a long time to mature, and by the time you do, the people you're supposed to be maturing for are generally gone.

There are two sides to me: the ornament and the orphan. The ornament continues to do all of these things, but the orphan, the core, anxiously seeks to catch up, to find an opening so he can raise his hand, speak forcefully, and say, "Let me be a part of you again!" When they do interact, we'll see what kind of person they create together. It's similar to Germany's reunification-will it be a noble country this time, or are all the misgivings that the cynical portion expresses true?

Will the question "Where is the compassion?" still be asked when the orphan and the ornament become one person? Will the response be, "Holy shit, there isn't any"?

Will you have toiled through a whole book, an entire life, to discover decency beneath the adornment, to see these parts together and ask "Who's really home?" and get the answer: "A serial killer, that's all." The completion, the merging-it was hopeless, and all of the amazing characteristics you were searching for in the melding of the halves were just wiped out, your worst fears realised.

I'm still perplexed. And I'm terrified of realising that the emotional anaesthetic I've been using will never be able to let the orphan take the lead and have a life of its own. I've frequently considered what a terrible liability it would be for someone to become an actor who is distant and anaesthetised, like I am.

I've always felt like a spectator of my own life. I'm not sure if the Budweisers contributed to this. I feel like I'm watching something but not living it. It's like gazing at an out-of-focus snapshot when the camera is rattled and the head is hazy. In fact, depending on how it has been vibrating, you can practically see three or four unique images. It's eerie; I guess I'm always eerie.

When I'm working, I feel the most united, with no separate bits of me strewn about. I could be attempting to think of something clever, imaginative, or unique for my role. Whether I'm working alone or with a group of people following a script, I sense trust, which is unusual for me.

Still, acting provided me with a safe haven in which I could express my feelings without fear of being judged; I could always laugh and say, "Oh, that's not me, that's just the character." It was critical for me to find a release, even if it was through fiction-even if I couldn't achieve those feelings in my real life.

What causes a person to become incapacitated? That's what I'm curious about. Isn't it true that a person wishes to be anaesthetised in order to avoid feeling whatever sensations are available? It's not that you don't care; it's just that you're always watching and so distant that you can never get inside. The core has never had the chance to fly and explore its own curiosity. It had been dethroned by the adornment.

The core had no chance.

The fact that you believe you emit a specific colour of light has always amazed me. You are certain that you are a lovely guy, or that you are a nasty guy, or that you are extremely complicated; whatever it is, the light that people see is not the same light that you believe you are emitting. They perceive things very differently. It's intriguing to have something on one side of the page utterly contradict something on the other side of the page. It's entertaining theatre. It shows that there is no such thing as a clear picture. There is no single statement, or set of assertions, that defines a person. I believe that what identifies a person is a set of serious conflicts produced by splashes of colour. You have a painting as a result of this. You can locate sections of the painting that are worth looking at and others that are not worth looking at.

Uncertainties have always existed for me. I've always been in pain and required assistance. And one of the reasons I decided to go to therapy (on more than one occasion) was that I was horribly unperceptive and careless about a lot of things. I believed I could learn to perform in a more mature manner.

My treatment focused on my children, marriage, alcohol, acting, politics, and anything else that came to mind. You would scrutinise every action you take, and if you believe it is not well thought out, done without a strategy, or immature, you would attempt to correct it in some way.

I've always had the impression that I cater to appearances, that I drink too much, that I don't know how to identify myself, and hence can't define my children-all of these terrible aspects of my existence. I've always been a private person who requires the constant presence of others. The damage was done to me when I discovered what people were looking for was not me. Writers created the characters. The appeal was in the wit and competence of the authors, as well as the wit and ability of those who conducted the exploitation and selling. What the audience wanted had no resemblance to the ornamentation, let alone the orphan. Do people mistake me for William Faulkner's Ben Quick? Or Hud? Or how about Butch Cassidy? Or how about Frank Galvin in The Verdict? Or any of the previous roles I've had? It's a shell that's being photographed on screen, pursued by fans, and gaining all the attention. While the essence of who I am remains unexplored, uncomfortable, and unknowable.

Stewart Stern: Are you upset about anything right now?

Paul: I guess I'm upset about becoming older. I will not age gracefully.

I just have a few strong beliefs. I don't believe in the hereafter. I don't believe in the hereafter. I'm not a mystic or a believer in the supernatural. But I'm confident that this is only a warm-up. And when I die and they place me in that box in the ground, someone will cry, "Cut!" At that point, a producer will say, "Okay, let's go back to the number-one position, let's get the cameras back there and shoot that scene all over again." And my box will reopen, and another existence will be continued or pursued. I believe I will die seven or eight times.

Everything will turn out to be a joke.

Printed in Great Britain
by Amazon